Joseph W. Bebo
PO Box 762
Hudson, MA, 01749
Email: joewbebobooks@gmail.com
Editor: James Oliveri
Interior and Cover Design: Elyse Zielinski

Library of Congress Cataloging in – Publication Data
Joseph W. Bebo
In the Back of the Van /Joseph Bebo – First Edition

ISBN: 978-0-9982182-0-5
Non-fiction, autobiography; music

In The
Back Of The Van

The Story Of One
Unforgettable Summer...

Joseph W. Bebo

To Dad and his love of music, for making this story possible.

Prologue

In the summer of 1968, while I was going to school in Boston, Massachusetts, I played drums with Van Morrison. He had just recorded Brown Eyed Girl and was in Boston trying to get out of his contract with Bang Records. While in town he put a band together, which I had the good fortune to play in. From Early June, soon after school got out for the semester, until late August when Van went to New York to record Astral Weeks, I worked with him every day, rehearsing and playing around town and the Cape. It was a critical time in Van's life and a turning point in mine. This is the story.

Chapter 1

The Audition

"Hey, Joey! Want a gig?"

It was 1968. I was twenty years old and had just finished my second year at Berklee College of Music in Boston. It was a day like any other in late May. Summer was in the air. The Sox were playing at Fenway on their way to the AL pennant and the World Series. It would have been a good day to be alive except that my parents had just told me they'd no longer be able to support me while I was going to school. The rent was due, the well had dried up, and I had no idea what to do. Little did I know, I would not only have money for the rent, I was about to have the most unforgettable summer of my life.

I was standing on the corner of Mass Ave and Boylston pondering my dilemma. I had already missed two turns of the light and was waiting for a third. I looked up and saw a friend from school crossing the street in my direction, a bass player named Tom Kielbania.

Tom and I had done some gigs together with pick-up bands working the seedier clubs around town. He had long, dark, unkempt hair that hung straight and limp like greasy spaghetti, and wore dark glasses morning, noon, and night, but he was the nicest guy you'd ever want to meet.

"Hey, Tom! What's up, man?" I asked in greeting, as he came across the street.

"You want a gig?" he repeated, stepping on the curb and nearly being side-swiped by an angry driver as he crossed against the light.

That's like asking a school boy if he wants the day off.

"Sure, where? How much? I hope it's not that last band we worked with. That guitar player almost got us thrown in the brig."

Our last job at the NCO club in the Charlestown Naval Yard had been a total disaster. Not only did we not get paid, we were escorted off the base by angry-eyed MPs who stood tapping their palms with the shafts of their clubs as we packed our equipment into the car.

"So what's up with Kevin?" I asked. The blond-haired, athletic-looking guitar player who had almost passed out on stage was responsible for the whole fiasco. "Was he high on something or what?"

6

"Yeah, smack."

"Great," I said. "Do me a favor and tell me the gig's not with that idiot."

"No, this is with Van Morrison!"

"Who?" I said.

"You know, the guy who did *Brown Eyed Girl*."

"Haven't heard it," I told him.

I was heavy into jazz at the time, although I was starting to listen to some of the newer rock coming on the scene, like the Beatles', *Rubber Soul* and Jimmy Hendrix, and of course, soul music. For some reason Van Morrison wasn't on my radar screen, although I would have recognized the tune after a few bars. It was a big hit.

"You've heard of *Gloria*, haven't you?" he asked, taking out a cigarette and lighting it up. "You know, the band Them?"

"That's teenybopper stuff," I said. "Don't tell me we're going to be playing for a bunch of teenyboppers."

"Yep."

"Sounds good! When do we start?" I replied.

Gloria was probably my least favorite song next to *Wipe Out*. The bland, monotonous beats bored me blind. I considered that 'garage band' stuff below me, but it sounded like that's what I'd be playing. Well, I needed a gig. My parents, although still paying my tuition, had just cut me off. It was a rude awakening. College meant everything to me and losing the opportunity to go to Berklee was just not an option. Now here Tom was offering me a gig on a silver platter. Things were starting to look up.

"We're rehearsing this afternoon," Tom told me as we walked back toward the dorm.

This was only a couple of years after Berklee had moved from its original location on Newbury Street up to the end of Boylston, just before the Fens.

"You can audition then," Tom continued. "I was just going over to the dorm to look for you. You were the first guy I thought of when Louie told us he had another gig."

"Oh, yeah, I heard Louie was playing with Charlie," I said. "They're doing an album. That lucky stiff, I'd give anything to play with Charlie Mariano."

Louie Peterson was another friend of ours from Berklee, who had been working with Van that spring and had just played an outdoor concert with him on the Common. Louie was a good player with a smooth, poppy style. He could really make a show band sizzle. He had recently done a TV date with the great jazz saxophonist Charley Mariano. Charley must have liked his playing, because he asked him to do a recording with him. I would have sold my sister for the job. Instead, I had to settle for this rock cat from some teenybopper band called, Them.

"Well, Van needs a drummer fast, someone who can pick up the tunes quick and play them down, keep a groove going and make it cook."

"You came to the right place," I replied, slapping him on the back. "Let me buy you a beer later. You pay."

"I'll have one now. You pay."

I couldn't turn him down.

Two beers and an hour later we were driving down Mass Ave to Cambridge in Tom's third-hand wreck to the audition. My drums and Tom's amp were stuffed in the back seat, all loaded in undue haste because we had spent too much time yapping and drinking. I had a little buzz on and hoped I wouldn't drop my sticks. I guess I'm really not much of a drinker. To make matters worse, Tom pulled out a hay-bar rolled to perfection with just a little bit of leaf peaking out of the tip of it. He lit it up and instantly filled the car up with acrid smelling smoke.

"Cripe, Tom!" I yelled. "Are you crazy? At least let me get the job before I get stoned and lose it."

"Don't be a candy-ass," he replied, handing me the joint.

We arrived wrecked out of our minds at the house where Van was rehearsing, a rather large Victorian place just off Harvard Square, the home of the seventeen-year-old guitar player, John Sheldon. A few more rooms and the place would have been a mansion. How we found it I'll never know. As we unloaded the equipment John came out to help.

To me, hardly knowing who he was and unimpressed with his songs, it was just another gig and Van just another band leader. It was a means to an end, keeping my apartment until school started in the fall. Little did I know that it would mark a milestone in my life.

I have no idea how Van put this group together, but we were about the weirdest looking bunch of characters you'd ever want to meet. John was just seventeen, tall and thin with gaunt features and long straight hair. He wore thick-lens, wire-rimmed glasses and had on a blue blazer. He reminded me of a preppy vampire. But then I was no

8

picnic either, with long, thick black hair, oversized sideburns, and a mustache that covered my entire upper lip. I must have looked like a pirate in my orange and purple striped t-shirt and bell-bottom pants. With Tom and his dumpy looks and frumpy clothes, always in shades, the three of us made the Nairobi Trio [1] look normal.

Somehow it all jelled that first day at the audition. Call it chemistry, call it luck, call it what you will, we all seemed to hit it off. John appeared nice enough and helped us lug the equipment into his basement where Van was waiting.

"You're late," he said to Tom. "You should have been here half an hour ago."

"I found a drummer," Tom informed him, "a good one too. Van this is Joey Bebo."

Van turned and looked at me. He was short, five-six or seven, with long, reddish hair and sharp, distinctive features. He was wearing a dark-green velvet jacket.

"Nice to meet you," he said in an Irish accent.

"Hi," I said, taking my bass drum out of its case and setting it down in the general area I intended setting up.

"You from Berklee?" he asked. He stood watching me like a bird of prey as I set up my kit.

"Yeah, same as Louie, we're in some of the same workshops."

We talked about music. He asked me what kind I liked and I mentioned my preference for jazz. He said he liked John Coltrane and seemed to know a lot about the idiom. My impression of the guy suddenly improved. Maybe this gig won't be so bad after all, I thought. Then we started playing - *Gloria*.

I recognized the tune instantly and knew the groove, so I was able to lay down the rhythm, emphasizing each of the four beats in the measure on my snare, using a lot of rim, while I kicked with the bass, trying to give it a little edge. There wasn't much I could do with it. In spite of my lack of regard for the tune, I had to admit it was a big hit. You could hardly go anywhere without hearing it on the radio or playing at some dance. So I was familiar with it and able to play it down without any trouble, but I was so bored I almost yawned.

---

[1] For those of you who don't remember, it's an old Ernie Kovacs bit with three guys dressed in gorilla suits playing in a marimba band that end up hitting each other instead of the marimbas.

As I may have mentioned, I was something of a musical snob at the time. If it wasn't jazz or serious soul, I just wasn't interested. Not that I couldn't play other kinds of music. I could play anything, and did. You had to just to make a living. If you weren't versatile, you weren't working.

During the song, I never took my eyes off Van, watching him for tempo and dynamics. He ignored me completely and really got into it. I kept the beat steady and tried to make it rock. Van appeared to like it well enough. At least I ended on time and it was somewhat recognizable as the thing he wrote. *Gloria* would remain my least favorite tune of Van's repertoire. Then again, perhaps this outlook helped me keep things in perspective, which was more important than I knew. Things got a little better when we did *Brown Eyed Girl*.

Even though I hadn't recognized the title when Tom mentioned it earlier, I knew the tune the minute we started playing. Following Tom's bass line, I laid down a snapping backbeat, working some syncopation into it with my bass drum while I rode my closed hi-hat. With John's heavy rock guitar line, however, it came out sounding like Jimmy Hendrix meets Bob Marley. It wasn't a bad tune, but after the third chorus I was more than ready for it to end. Van seemed to like my playing, but I was ready to trade Van Morrison for Charlie Mariano.

This just goes to show you what a fool I was. Here I was playing a piece of music that was destined to become a rock and roll classic and I couldn't wait for it to end. Van was standing right there not six feet away singing his heart out with these beautifully contrived lyrics and melody, and I wanted to trade places with Louie. But it was a gig, and by the looks of it a good one. I'd had to play a lot worse things to make a living, from backing up strippers with bump and grind, to playing society music for the rich and senile. It was all the same to me. A gig was a gig was a gig. I could play the music I liked on my own time. For now I had to make a living. My parents had just cut me off.

As we played Van's song, I dazed off, replaying the terrible phone call of earlier that day in my head.

"We just can't continue to support you in Boston and pay for your tuition," my dad informed me. "You're going to have to shoulder some of the burden if you want to go to school. Anyway, your mother tells me you've been smoking pot. If you have money to buy dope, you can support yourself down there. You've upset your mother very much."

I felt like I had been kicked in the stomach, like someone had taken the floor and swept it out from under me. My rent alone would break me in a month. Reality hit me like a wall of water, almost sweeping away my fragile composure.

"It was just that one time," I mumbled pathetically. I hung up the phone as if I'd just been told I had seven days to live.

Somehow I managed to end the tune with the others, although it was more luck than instinct. I may not have appreciated the music, but I sure needed the job. Luckily, I happened to be playing well that afternoon in spite of myself. At least Van wasn't throwing my drums out onto the street.

I love the song *Brown Eyed Girl* now. I could listen to it all day. Every time I hear it I stop what I'm doing. I've come to recognize it for the great classic that it is, probably destined to outlive us all. My musical elitism has left me over the years as I and the music itself have evolved. At the time, however, he only had these two hits, *Gloria* and *Brown Eyed Girl*. I hoped my face wouldn't betray my apathy. Van didn't seem to notice because he ended up hiring me.

Now, you may be wondering how a guy like me, who wasn't really a 'rock' player could get a job with Van Morrison. That's a good question. I had a jazzy, modern style that could make a band pop. I could get downright funky, especially when I had a good bass player to work with like Tom. For me feel was everything. If it didn't feel right, I didn't like it. Van always played with a lot of feeling, even during rehearsals. He was that kind of guy. He had soul.

We continued playing all afternoon. Van hadn't said anything but I assumed I had the gig. He sang and played harmonica. Sometimes he'd pick up a guitar and strum the rhythm he'd want to hear. We were having a good jam. He even blew a squeaky solo on the sax. I had no idea what the songs were. I never could pick up the lyrics or the titles, and I wasn't much interested. I had all I could do just keeping it all together, following Tom's bass while John wailed away on the guitar, sometimes in tune, but always generating plenty of feedback and energy. We played down a few cover tunes, bluesy stuff, which I vaguely recognized.

Van seemed pretty easy going. As a matter of fact, in all the time I knew him I seldom heard him say more than a few sentences at a time. He didn't really seem comfortable around people, but he was absolutely great to work with. He certainly didn't say much that first rehearsal. He never complained or found fault with anything we did, a rarity in the ego-saturated rock and roll business where everyone is a prima donna and thinks they're God's gift to music. Whatever we did that first day seemed to be good enough for Van. Not that we sounded that bad.

Van left it to me to figure out what kind of rhythms to play. Other than to count down the tunes he didn't say much through the whole rehearsal. I don't remember him ever telling us what to play or providing much direction. Somehow, though, we seemed to all hit on something after the first few bars. Come to think of it, we hardly varied these songs much from that first time we did them, even after working together all summer. Something just clicked. You had to feel it, and that was OK with me.

The rest of the rehearsal went well. For some reason the three of us, with our divergent styles and musical backgrounds, worked well together. We had a raw, high-energy edge that blended nicely with Van's voice. It was a unique sound that was fun to play. It was more like a jam session than a rehearsal. Van was like one of the guys, and the band cooked. We played down a number of interesting songs that afternoon, and by the end of the rehearsal I had a new found appreciation for the man and his music. He was the real deal.

When we were through and I was tearing down my drums, he came over.

"You sounded good. You've got the job if you want it," he confirmed.

"Great! Nice tunes," I said. "That was fun."

"I'll pay you $150 a week for rehearsals and $150 a performance. I want to rehearse the band here for a couple weeks then start playing the clubs around town."

"Sounds good! When do we start?"

"Ten o'clock tomorrow."

I was elated. Not only was I making more money in a single show than I usually picked up playing seven nights and weekend matinees, but I'd get paid for rehearsals, a thing unheard of in the types of bands I worked with. What started out as a disastrous summer was turning out to be a good one after all.

"Good job," said Tom, as we drove home together that evening.

"Yeah, that was fun. It'll be good playing with you all summer, nothing like a good bass player to make life easy."

"Yeah, thanks. We had a good grove going there."

"So, what's the story with this guy? If he's such a big rock star what's he doing here in Boston playing with us, eh?"

"I guess he's having some legal hassles with his old record company in New York, Bang Record, bunch of heavies. Van said they ripped him off. He didn't make a cent for *Brown Eyed Girl* and it sold millions. He's getting a band together while he hires some big Boston lawyer to get him out of his contract. In the meantime, he can't record or anything."

"No kidding. Well his misfortune is our good luck, buddy. We got us a gig for the summer. How did you hook up with him?"

"Louie found me practicing my bass in one of the rooms at school. Told me he was playing with a great singer who needed a bass player. I didn't know who Van was at first, but I recognized the tunes."

"Same here, but he seems to be on the level."

"Yeah, we're going to be rich and famous, man."

"Alleluia, brother! Alleluia!"

Chapter 2

Joey - the Early Years

You may wonder what led me to this point in my life, to this milestone in the relatively mundane, obscure existence to which I would soon return. It was a life full of music.

I grew up in upstate New York, in a small city called Plattsburgh, at the northeastern-most tip of the state along scenic Lake Champlain, which explains a lot if you've ever been there. With a SAC Air Force base and a fair-sized state college, it was quite a cosmopolitan place for a little town of 24,000 or so stuck in the middle of nowhere. That's what it felt like to me, nowhere. I couldn't wait to get out of there and always dreamed of living in some big city.

As small as it was, the town and surrounding vicinity was a source of rich musical experiences. Lake Placid was nearby, as was Burlington, Vermont and Montreal in Canada, and great names in jazz and big bands came through the area frequently, including Buddy Rich, Duke Ellington, Count Basie, Cozy Cole, and Louis Armstrong, to name a few.

My early musical influences were naturally derived from my parents, who loved music of all kinds, country, swing, pop, Latin. They never lost an opportunity to take us to see any big name performers who came within a couple hours of our home.

My dad bought my first drum set when I was ten years old, a real kit, with a large, twenty-four inch bass drum and a little red snare. The bass drum had a small cymbal connected to it, with a woodblock and a cowbell attached, a real little drummer's menagerie. It was Christmas 1958. I'll never forget that first big bass drum with the dancing hula girl painted on the front of it. Boy, could I make her vibrate!

Until then if I wanted to play the drums I had to turn all my mother's pots and pans upside down on the kitchen counter, along with her glass and metal ashtrays, which I used as cymbals. I would bang on these all day to the music on the record player like a tiny Tasmanian devil, using a couple wooden spoon handles.

My younger brother, Jim, had asked for a guitar, but I knew the drums were for me. I realized that with those other instruments you had to learn notes. With drums all you had to do was sit down and start playing to the beat, and that's what I did the first time I saw them.

There was a song playing on the record player - which there was through most of the time we were growing up - a Fats Waller tune called, *Blueberry Hill*. Somehow I knew the song called for brushes. So I picked up the pair sitting on my brand new drum set and started swirling them around on the snare, slapping the rhythm with my right hand, as if I had been doing this all my life, although I don't recall at this early date ever seeing anyone do it. I had no problem playing along with the music and keeping the beat, adding the bass drum on the downbeat and the hi-hat on the upbeat– not much more than little brass cups that clanged together when I pushed the pedal. Somehow it all came intuitively, probably from playing my mother's pots and pans along with all kinds of music. My parents were amazed.

Our radio and record player were constantly playing. My parents loved music. Latin music, standards, big bands, Dixieland, music from the Hit Parade, my folks listened to it all. One of their favorites was Louie Prima and Keely Smith. My father even had a collection of original Benny Goodman and Gene Krupa records, which included the famous Carnegie Hall concert featuring *Sing, Sing, Sing*.

Dad used to play guitar and sing funny, folksy songs. He also played the harmonica, pretty well if I recall. Sometimes he'd hang the harp around his neck so he could play it while he strummed the guitar. He would sing and play those funny old tunes and put us in stitches. That was about the extent of my family's prior musical involvement.

Whenever I heard someone playing a drum solo, I would imagine it was me. I played along with Gene Krupa and Cozy Cole, and could soon play their rather simple beats and solos. Same with the Dixieland records, which always had drum solos, but it was Buddy Rich who made the biggest impression on me and first made me really want to be a drummer.

The first time I heard a Buddy Rich solo I couldn't believe my ears. It absolutely blew my mind. I listened to that solo over and over again. He made it sound like there were five guys playing he hit so many drums and cymbals so fast! It brought tears to my eyes. I so much wanted to be able to do that, but I had a slight problem. As much as I liked playing the drums, I hated practicing.

My first drum teacher was a gentleman called Nap Light. He had the top dance band in town and played in the pit orchestra for the summer stock shows they did at the college, so he was a schooled musician. My father used to say he had the best beat of any drummer in town, because he didn't speed up or slow down, and he never miss a beat, which meant he was easy to dance to.

Nap dutifully tried to teach me my rudiments and how to read. Reading was easy enough, quarter notes, eighth notes, sixteenth notes and so on. No problem there. Rudiments were another thing entirely. The *single-stroke* and *double-stroke rolls*, the *flames* and the *paradiddles* and *flamacues,* and so on, are the very foundation of percussion instruments, as important to drumming as scales are to every other instrument. I just didn't get it.

OK, you can use *double-strokes* and *single-strokes* and *paradiddle*-like strokes to move around the drums. To me, probably because I learned these basics by playing along with other drummers, it was all just about beating out a rhythm I could move my hands all over my make-shift drum sets, playing all sorts of strokes, and mimic the solos I heard – all except Buddy Rich's that is. I didn't need to sit and practice these repetitive patterns over and over on a drum pad – or so I thought.

After a few months of fruitlessly trying to get me to learn my rudiments, which meant playing them smoother and faster each time he saw me, Nap gave up.

"Your *double-stroke roll* sounds like potatoes rolling down stairs," he announced one day during my lesson.

He probably said it to shame me into practicing more, but I thought it was the funniest thing I ever heard. I wasn't ashamed or offended. He was right. It was a perfectly apt description of my pathetic *double-stroke roll,* but I didn't care. When I needed to, for short bursts, my *double-stroke roll* was good enough. Who wanted to stand there playing rolls all day? I made the mistake of laughing.

After he left my parents informed me that Nap had told them they were wasting their money on drum lessons for me, and that suited me fine. Nap was right, and being the gentleman that he was, didn't want to take my parents' hard earned money for something I wasn't interested in – learning rudiments. He wouldn't be the last drum teacher - some of who, like Nap, were very good - to drop me as a student. Now I was left free to just wail away on my drum set. I felt liberated.

Over the years my drum set got more sophisticated and expensive, and I built up solos, playing along to my favorite swing, Dixieland, and jazz bands. My musical tastes also grew more sophisticated.

My parents loved Latin music, so I was constantly exposed to those beats as well. Xavier Cugat, Mongo Santamaria, and Tito Puente, I used to love playing along to those hot Latin bands. Then Dave Brubeck came along.

I always listened to the drummer first. If I didn't like the drummer, I didn't like the band. Joe Morello was definitely something different. His drums had quite a unique sound, and the type of music they were playing was distinctive as well, all in different time signatures – 5/4, 7/8, 12/4. It was mind-boggling. Joe Morello could make it all swing. From Dave Brubeck and Joe Morello I eventually made the switch to hardcore jazz.

I built my set up one drum at a time. First a real top-of-the-line snare to replace the little red toy one, then a tom tom to hang on my big bass drum. Next a floor tom, and finally a new twenty inch bass drum to replace the old twenty-four inch one - though I missed that hula girl - all white pearl Ludwigs. I also added three Zildjian cymbals - a splash and two rides – and a new, deluxe hi-hat, which I could use with my left foot to play the off-beat, or bang on closed for rock and Latin tunes.

I used to set my drums up in the garage and play solos for the neighborhood kids. I would unleash my latest creation – a hodge-podge of solos I heard from Cozy Cole and Gene Krupa, to Dixieland and Latin beats, all ingeniously woven together in my inimitable fashion, my bass drum pounding out every beat in a steady 4/4 time, while I banged the life out of every last drum, all four of them – and cymbals – with everything I was worth, using accents and rim-shots to spice things up. The sound would come booming out of the concrete confines of the garage and echo over the neighborhood like an artillery barrage. The kids would come from blocks around to listen – their parents too - sitting on the lawn and driveway in front of the house. The children clapped and laughed. The grownups asked me how I learned to do that. I didn't know how to answer them. I didn't learn it. I just did it. I must have been around twelve or thirteen.

Because I listened to so many drum solos, I just didn't bang on the skins. I played them, always carrying the beat. I was a musical drummer and inventive. I would keep up a beat, but constantly vary it in subtle ways, trying to make it interesting, using double-strokes and single-strokes as fills, accenting with rim-shots, interspersing toms with snare and cymbals to add variety, using dynamics for effect. It was unusual for someone that age. I didn't work up solos as some drummers do, but made it up as I went, never playing the same thing twice. If asked to repeat what I did I probably couldn't have except for the basic beat.

Somewhere along the line someone with a rock band heard me. They needed a drummer for a dance and called my parents. I'd never played in a real band before, but I had played along with enough of them. I couldn't have been much over fourteen. It was my first gig. I remember it well. It was at the Teen Center out on a place called Cumberland Head. Everyone else in the band was much older, practically grownups, and it was all rock and roll. Rock was one of the few types of music I never played along with because the drumming was usually so simple, but like everything else when it came to drums, it all came naturally. I just followed along with the other instruments, pounding out the beat with my bass drum and smashing the backbeat with my left hand on the snare, while riding and crashing the cymbals for all they were worth, filling in with runs up and down the skins to kick in the next section. It must have sounded OK, because everyone was on the dance floor sweating up a storm. Even then I could keep a beat. They hired me back to play at the County Fair.

Even though Nap gave up on me, I learned to read music and play the rudiments well enough to get into the high school band at Mount Assumption Institute, an all boy academy run by the Catholic Brothers of Religious Instruction. I wasn't quite in high school yet, being only an eighth grader, but I was in their preparatory school at St. Peter's so they let me audition.

The band director at that time was an old gentleman in his seventies named Peter 'Sarge' Blessant. He was renowned in the area for his concert bands, which always won highest marks in the state competitions. This occurred all the years I was in the band, before his retirement.

I was just about the youngest kid in the orchestra, and certainly the shortest, but I got to play snare drum right off. No cymbal, bass drum, or triangle for me. I learned how to play in an orchestra from one of the best directors in the area. How to watch the conductor for cues and dynamics, when to play loud and when to play soft, and my *double-stroke roll* was good enough when played with all the other drummers and instruments that no one complained. We played concerts all over the state.

What really made it special was when, in my very first year in high school, as a freshman, despite being the youngest percussionist, Peter Blessant picked me for the dance band. I didn't think much of it at the time. After all, I was just playing along having fun, doing what I always did, but apparently it was unprecedented for someone so young. One of the other parents objected that their boy, who had played in it the year before and had been in the band much longer, should be in the dance band. Besides, he would soon be graduating. Peter Blessant was not a man to be dictated to, however. He told them that I could swing the band, their son couldn't, and that was that. From listening and playing along to all those swing bands, I knew how to fill-in and kick the accents. My dad used to say I made you jump in your seat.

As a fourteen year old kid, just in ninth grade, I was playing at senior proms all around town and the surrounding area. We played standards and swing tunes, even sambas, rumbas, and cha-chas. Some of the charts were pretty demanding, but I had no trouble reading them. Most of the time, I could just feel it. We had no bass player, but that didn't bother me and my big fat bass drum foot thumping out the beat in four-four time, or sometimes in three. From then on, all through high school I played in the school dance bands.

In my second year at MAI two other drummers, who were really exceptional players, joined the band. Dave Curtin – now deceased - was probably one of the best rudimentary drummers I have ever known. Where my *single-stroke roll* was pretty pathetic, Dave's sounded like a smooth whisper, and his *paradiddles* were a thing of marvel. He had a chest full of medals from All-State competitions. The other drummer was a boarder at the school from New England, named Guy Danais – he beat me out of a job years later while we were at Berklee together. He too had a snappy, crisp military style and very good hands. Despite their skills with the sticks, however, I still got the dance band seat – I could swing the band.

It was great playing with Dave and Danais. Even though our styles were different, we played well together. It was probably the strongest drum section I have ever been in. I used to love marching in parades with these two. We'd dream up these hip cadences, which we would play while the band marched silently in parade or during football games, while we maneuvered to positions on the field. We'd march that band along like high-stepping Lipizzaners, much to the consternation of the veteran groups in front of us. More than one organization complained that we were marching too fast, but we loved those snappy military cadences, which we played with exuberance. That's the way old 'Sarge' liked it.

The high point of my small town musical life was when a kid name Rick Austin asked me to form a group with him and another young musician by the name of Jerry LaVene – now deceased. The name of the band was, The Teenaged Jazzmen, and together, you could say we made North Country history.

Rick was a year ahead of me in school and lived a couple of streets away. He played piano, but it was the clarinet that he played almost exclusively with us. Jerry was a child prodigy on the guitar. Even as a kid he was one of the best guitarists in the area. He had an unbelievably sophisticated harmonic knowledge and an incredible ear, even for a twenty-year-old, and he was only fourteen.

The three of us, clarinet, guitar, and drums made quite a combo. We played Dixieland and swing tunes – the *Saints Go Marching In* and *Sing Sing Sing* were a couple of our favorites – but also standards and Dave Brubeck compositions like *Take Five* and *Pick up Sticks*. We even did some rock – Beatles songs and soul. We debuted at the opening of the West End Shopping Center, the first mall in Plattsburgh, not far from where I lived.

Over the next few years we must have played a hundred gigs around the area, high school proms and dances, local nightspots like the Cadillac Club and Holiday Inn, the Elks Club and the Knights of Columbus. You name it, we played it. My dad brought us to and from every single job. He did the booking as well, and we worked steady, at least two or three weekends a month.

One of the most memorable places we performed was the New York State Prison in Dannemora, NY. I'll never forget walking through the corridors to the concert hall, hearing the doors clanging shut behind me. I saw some of the scariest looking hombres I had ever seen there. I mean, if looks could kill, and we had to play to a whole auditorium of them.

The place was packed to the rafters with men in blue denim, the guards ringing the room and on catwalks above. Talk about a captive audience. Beings kids we weren't nervous at all, and started with our favorite song, *sing, sing, sing*. It brought down the house. Boy did they love drum solos. I must have done a half-dozen of them before we were done our two-hour set. They asked us back for a second command performance. I have to say they were the most appreciative audience I have ever played for.

You have to love my parents. Can you imagine what it must have been like with me banging my drums in the garage, and before that on pots and pans in the living room, morning, noon, and night? Not once did they ever complain about the noise or tell me to be quiet. They were very encouraging. Until then all my musical influence had come from them, the Dixieland, the Latin music, the swing bands and top-40 songs, even Dave Brubeck, all of it. I had never bought a record on my own except for a Chubby Chucker forty-five of the Twist for a party when I was twelve.

My musical awakening occurred when I walked into the record shop in the middle of downtown Plattsburgh. It must have been somewhere between my fifteenth and sixteenth birthdays. It was on Court Street just across from the Strand Theater and they had an incredible jazz selection, very hip for a small town, probably because we hosted a SAC air force base with plenty of afficianodos from the City. I was literally like a kid in a candy store.

I had plenty of cash to burn. My group, the Teenaged Jazzmen, made $150 a gig between the three of us. Fifty dollars a week was good money back then for a kid to be making. Sometimes we worked back to back dates, and on New Years Eve we made $100 apiece. I must have dropped $80 a month in that store, all of it on Jazz records. That place treated me like royalty when I walked in. I could sit in a booth all day with headphones on sampling records and no one complained – and listen I did!

I discovered a whole world of music no one had told me about. John Coltrane, Miles Davis, Charles Mingus, Dizzy and Bird, I found them all just following my ears. Art Blakey and the Jazz Messengers, Milt Jackson and the Modern Jazz Quartet, Max Roach, Philli-Jo Jones and Elvin Jones, they all knocked my socks off. The 'cool' big band sounds of Thad Jones, Quincy Jones, and Gil Evans were all there waiting for me to pick them up like gold nuggets in a stream. There was Stan Getz and Charlie Bird, Jimmy Smith and Richard Groove Holmes, Stanley Turrentine, Herbie Mann, Sonny Rowland, Sonny Stitt, Cannonball Adderly, Roland Kirk, Kenny Burrell; Donald Bird, Joe Pass, Paul Chambers, Oscar Peterson, George Shearing, Nancy Wilson, Sarah Vaughn, Tony Williams, McCoy Tyner; Ray Brown, Reggie Workman, Charley Mclean, Ornette Coleman, Billy Higgins, Jimmy Cobb, Ahmad Jamal, Herbie Hancock, Freddy Hubbard, Maynard Fergerson, I had all their albums, and these are just the ones I remember off the top of my head. They all became my friends and idols. I listened to these albums night and day, using earphones I bought so I could continue late in the evenings without disturbing anybody. My parents became concerned because I spent so much time in my room, but I had discovered another world, a whole new universe of sounds. I must have listened to Coltrane's Crescent album a thousand times. By the time I got to Berklee I had a jazz collection second to none. There would be guys going back and forth from my dorm room that first year all the time borrowing my vinyl and sometimes even bringing them back.

By the age of sixteen I had quite a reputation as a drummer and was being asked to play in all sorts of groups, mostly with grownups. I played resorts and night clubs from Lake Placid and Saranac Lake to Montreal and Burlington, not to mention the NCO and Officers' clubs at the Air Force Base. Along the line I worked with some of the North Country's finest musicians, all before my seventeenth birthday. I thought I was the pretty good. Boy was I in for a rude awakening.

There's nothing more humbling than coming to the big city and a place like Berklee. It really opened my eyes. When I got to Boston I saw how really good some people could play, guys like Joe Labara and Harvey Mason, two amazing drummers, who were both in my class. It was then that I realized I should have practiced my rudiments more.

A little before I went off to college, I got to meet one of the all time greats of jazz, Mister Louis Armstrong. It was the summer of 1964. It was his 64th birthday and a centennial celebration for the town of Plattsburgh. This was soon after the *Hello Dolly* album and he brought his band to town to play. We had seen Louie in Lake Placid a few years earlier, and I became sort of a pen pal with his drummer, Danny Barcelona, who was a good Dixieland player. My parents owned a motel near the beach at the time and when they heard Louis Armstrong was coming to town, they wrote Danny and invited them to stay at our place. They accepted. The whole band was there, Billy Kyle, the pianist, Big Chief Russell Moore, the trombonist, Danny, Louie, sitting right in our living room lobby like part of the family. I even put on a concert of my own for them, inviting two of the North Country's best young musicians, Fred Lewis, Plattsburgh's version of Richie Cole, and my guitar playing buddy from the Teenage Jazzmen, Jerry Levene. My brother Jim played bass. We got down, doing tunes like *Night in Tunisia*, *Giant Steps,* and *Round About Midnight*, taking them out. Mister Armstrong just smiled politely and said nothing. The others ignored us and talked among themselves, but Danny Barcelona and their female singer - whose name I've forgotten but who made the biggest impression on this seventeen year old boy - were surprised to find teenagers playing that kind of music in Plattsburgh, New York.

We drove Louie to the concert in Dad's secondhand Caddy. You should have seen the faces of our friends when we got out of that car with Louis Armstrong. My youngest brother, Jess, carried his trumpet for him. After the concert they came back to the motel and sat in the lobby talking. We had his album, *Hello Dolly*, playing on the stereo. Louie listened to that song over and over again until he fell asleep in his chair. We have a picture of him sleeping on our lazy boy with a piece of birthday cake on his plate. Needless to say it's a priceless family heirloom. A lot of people nowadays don't even know who he is, or only know him for his singing, but in his day, in the twenties and thirties, no one had heard anything coming out of a trumpet like Louis Armstrong could play it. He redefined the instrument and influenced generations of horn players, and even then, at sixty-four, he still blew a mean Dixieland trumpet. Talk about a consummate entertainer, he was the tops in my book.

By the time I got the job with Van I had two years of Berklee under my belt and no longer wanted to be just an entertainer. I thought of myself as an artist. I was about to work with one of the best songwriters and singers of all time and I didn't have a clue. It was just a gig.

Chapter 3

The Electric Band

Bright and early the morning after the audition, I arrived at John's house for rehearsal. I wasn't used to playing before 9:00 pm, so I had a little trouble getting loosened up. By the afternoon, though, we were warmed up and cooking with gas. Van brought out a number of songs we hadn't done the previous day, which we played down with just as much ease. I still couldn't understand a syllable of the lyrics. I seldom bothered finding out their titles, but the tunes were nice and I was starting to enjoy myself.

One of the songs that I remember doing a lot that summer was *Domino*. This was long before it came out on one of Van's album. He was still developing it, and left plenty of room for us to play around in. I gave it a Bo Diddley beat, working my snare and bass drum against John's rhythmic guitar hook. We made it rock and shook the walls of that small basement room.

Van is one of those people you only have to listen to for a few seconds to recognize, his voice is so distinctive. The more I listened to him, the more I appreciated his singing. This impression has only grown over the years as I've watched him evolve and his music progress.

During a brief lunch break, after John's mother brought down sandwiches and soft drinks, we went out to his spacious, hedge-lined backyard and threw a Frisbee around. Van, still in his green velvet jacket with a can of beer in his hand, joined us, but had trouble throwing the saucer-shaped object without it spiraling to the ground in front of him. John had on a white shirt as if he was going to church and leapt around the yard like a gazelle, snatching the thing in mid air. Tom hardly moved at all, except when he waddled back to retrieve a missed catch, which was often. Van talked about his plans.

"My agent's lining up gigs for next month. We're going to need twenty or thirty songs at least. We've got a lot of work to do."

It was all the same to me. I was being paid to play Frisbee.

I didn't know quite what to make of this little guy with the long red hair. He didn't act like a rock star. He was more like one of the guys, very unassuming. After a few more rounds of retarded Frisbee we went back inside and continued the rehearsal. The more I played, the more I began to listen to what the other guys were doing.

John had a raucous, hard rock sound that seemed out of place with Van's bluesy style, but he filled up the empty spaces like a fat man fills an airplane seat, with twangs and strums and plenty of feedback. You just never knew what to expect. Yet sometimes he could play tastefully and lyrically. He was the only one besides Van that seemed comfortable on stage, where he jumped around with the music, even during rehearsals, like he did playing Frisbee.

Tom was a solid bass player, with strong lines and good intonation. He always stood out distinctly no matter how loud John got. He could play jazz as well as rock, upright and electric with equal ease. Tom could do it all.

As I've said, I was mainly a jazz drummer playing rock and roll, though I played hard enough to fake it. I drummed with my head down, usually with a scowl or grimace on my face, as I concentrated on the music, trying to make things sizzle. I had no stage presence and little personality, and rarely if ever smiled. There was no way of telling if I was mad or just concentrating, a lot like Van, I guess. Our divergent styles were starting to blend as we worked away the hours in John Sheldon's basement.

I could hear Van's voice quite distinctly and noticed it had a special quality. He used it like a horn, with good power and range. He certainly cut through all the noise we were making. I was becoming a Van Morrison fan. Go figure.

Unfortunately, all the time I played with him I never listened to his lyrics, although I'm what you'd call a 'listening' drummer. I was too busy concentrating on what all the other instruments were doing, so I could kick with them as they accented this line or that rhythm. I heard Van's voice as another instrument, but not the lyrics, I'm sorry to say.

Every day found us learning new tunes and practicing old ones. Now and then Van would bring in something he wanted us to try out, usually just the words and chords. Although I was never sure what they were, I got the impression many of them were love songs to his wife, Janet. One of them was Moon Dance.

"Here, try this," he'd say, and hand out some loose-leaf sheets with chords and lyrics scribbled on them. "A tune I'm working on."

Whatever we were playing it wasn't jazz or folk. There was nothing acoustical about this band. Even in John's basement we used amps and speakers, and a PA. I don't remember playing soft, just the opposite. We were rehearsing for big halls and venues. Tom and I would lay down a steady, rocking rhythm and John would fill up the empty spaces with heavy but rhythmic guitar and feedback. At times we got into a nice groove. The group had an unusual mix of styles, heavy rock, jazz, and blues that ended up giving the band a unique blend. Add Van to the mix and you had something.

There were better drummers kicking around school than myself, and Tom certainly wasn't the best bass player at Berklee, but Van seemed to like what he heard. I'm not sure where he found John. As I've said, he was only seventeen at the time, but I found him rhythmical and fun to play with. Although talented for his age, I had worked with a lot better players at school. But John was the guy who had the gig and that was good enough for me. I was too busy trying to keep my end up to worry about critiquing the other musicians.

It's funny, when you're playing with a group like this you have to listen to the other musicians very closely, especially in jazz, so you can move with them as they play with the time and the changes. You have to know when to accent and when to fill, when to play loud and when to play soft, when to kick it and when to let it ride. Sometimes it's all written out for you, but much of the time you're just winging it, adlibbing, improvising. As closely as you listen to the other players, however, you can never hear it all together like it sounds to the listener from the outside. You miss the big picture. You're too involved. At one level you're listening to everyone else, but at another you're concentrating on what you're doing. So you can never fully appreciate the totality of what's going on. There are times, however, when you're in the zone and everything is working on its own, when you transcend yourself. It's almost like sitting in the audience wondering how those cats are doing it. Times like that are almost magical.

So I soon began to appreciate what Van was doing, and instantly liked the new tunes he introduced to the group, which gave us plenty of room to play our own rhythms and licks. Some of them were originals. No one had ever done these songs before, so it was pretty much wide open as to what we could do.

All this time, while we rehearsed, I considered it just another gig. I wasn't used to this band bonding thing, but I was getting paid for it so I went along. For two weeks we spent every day and most of the evenings together, either playing or talking about playing or listening to someone else play.

One day after rehearsal we went into nearby Harvard Square to have lunch. The four of us must have been quite a sight - John with his long-faced, scarecrow looks; Tom with his frumpy clothes and dark glasses - even though it was an overcast day; me with my colorful psychedelic shirt and pink-striped bell-bottoms; Van leading the way with his distinctive young Beethoven look. If we weren't in a band of some kind we sure should have been, that or the circus.

We crossed a park and approached the Square. It was a late spring afternoon, still warm at six. The street in front of the place was crowded with people. Instead of going into the restaurant, Van mingled with the crowd. Suddenly someone recognized him and stopped to get his autograph. Soon there was a throng around him. He stood calmly signing autographs and talking to folks, telling them he was playing around town. The rest of us disappeared into the background, as if we didn't exist. That's when it began to dawn on me that this might be more than just a gig.

Unbeknownst to any of us, except perhaps Van himself, this was a transition period for him. He was at a crossroad in his career, leaving Them and the Bang era and entering a new phase that would ultimately produce a string of hit albums spanning the early '70's to the present day, with many memorable songs that have touched thousands of lives all over the world and are now classics. It was part of music history, a once in a lifetime experience, and I didn't have the faintest idea.

Chapter 4

Berklee

There was never any doubt where I would go to college when I graduated from high school in 1966 - Berklee College of Music, the school of jazz. I remember driving down to Boston with my father to audition, and arriving at the school, which was still on Newbury Street at the time. It had just become accredited, so I would be in the first graduating class to get degrees in music education or composition. The former was going to be my major as a sop to my parents for going along with the decision. At least I could teach music if I didn't make it as a jazz musician, I told them, and they bought it.

Berklee's most famous graduate at the time was Quincy Jones, who was one of my favorite big band leaders and arrangers, along with Gil Evans. The fact that one of my idols had gone there made the place even more appealing.

I stepped out of the car and heard an unbelievable trumpet solo coming from a second story window, just blasting these incredible high, clean notes in a jazzy solo. Walking down the street toward the front entrance I heard this astounding tenor player sliding up and down some exotic scales as though it was Coltrane himself practicing, coming from the basement. I was entranced. This place was cooler than dry ice.

I was there again the following fall after passing an entrance exam on drums with Fred Buda, the drummer for the Pops, and a quiz by John Laporta – the saxophonist - on scales and reading, which I had also learned by this time.

The first day of Berklee was truly memorable, and humbling. There were auditions all week to determine who would get into what workshop with what famous Berklee faculty member, and there were many, from Phil Wilson and Charlie Mariano, to Herb Pomeroy and John LaPorta. Every so often someone would go into an audition room and suddenly you'd hear this incredible solo blasting out. This happened when Richie Cole auditioned, and when people who already had a name showed up, like Miroslav Vitous or Jann Hammer. Then you'd see a crowd gather around the door as if the President himself was auditioning.

In my hometown I was kind of a phenomenon, this little kid who could beat the heck out of the drums and comp the rhythm behind a hip adult jazz soloist. I thought I was pretty good until I got to Boston. Those first few days of auditions, listening to all those wonderful players, some who would soon be who's-who in the music world, was as intimidating as it was thrilling. As I've mentioned, drummers like Joe Labara and Harvey Mason were there at the time. These guys were – and still are - amazing players, not so much fast stickers like Buddy Rich, but superb musicians, instantly recognized by their unique and polished styles behind the drums. These two were just the tip of the drumming talent floating around that school when I got there. They were my peers - my competition - the elite club I would have to become part of if I were to succeed at my chosen profession. It was daunting.

I must have shown promise, because my first workshop was with Charlie Mariano. A full twelve piece band with some incredible players, including Richie Cole, Pat Labara, and Billy Pierce. That band cooked, but Charlie would interrupt us every other bar and complain about something - bad notes, poor intonation, *the time*! It could be a stressful hour and a half. We seldom got a chance to just play something down, but occasionally Charlie would pick up the alto and play with us. Boy did he wail. It would send chills up your spine. The sax section would sit there with tears in their eyes when he soloed. He could make that horn sing.

I'd get excited when I played with him and occasionally get carried away a bit, taking the time with me. When this happened, he'd glance up at me over his horn with a look that would freeze my blood and rein me in.

I guess Charley didn't care for my big band playing that much. The other drummer in the workshop got to go on to play in Phil Wilson's coveted band. I got Andy McGee, who was a good sax player in his own right, but not as coveted a workshop. I eventually did get into Phil's band, but I had a bit of development to go through first.

My first drum teacher at Berklee was a gentleman named Lou M., who played vibes at one of the hotels in town, so I picked up a little of that instrument as well. Lou put me on a regimen of sticking exercises, which included a lot of rudiments and wrist strengthening drills - as if I were an overweight recruit trying to make the cut – getting me ready for guys like Fred Buda and Alan Dawson. It must have worked, because after a couple of years I finally got to study with them as well.

Fred honed my reading skills and Allen developed my hand-foot coordination. They both continued with the hand calisthenics, all to a strictly ticking metronome – faster and faster.

During my time there I was fortunate to play with many wonderful musicians. Berklee was a literal cornucopia of soon to be jazz greats. So it was little wonder I was less than impressed with Van Morrison, at least initially.

By the summer of '68 I had finished my second year and was considering switching my major from Music Education to Music Composition and Arranging, especially after my parents had cut me off. I figured if I was going to be paying my way, I'd at least do it on my own terms. As a junior in education I'd be student teaching and taking theory courses. As a composition major I'd be getting into the cooler, more advanced musical curriculum, things like counterpoint with Bill Maloof and line-writing with Herb Pomeroy, as well as "serious" composition courses with instructors like John Bavicchi and Jeronimous Kachinkas.

First, I had to get through the summer.

Chapter 5

Getting to Know You

Even though Van was quiet and a bit hard to get to know, you can't help getting close to someone working with them every day for two months. When we weren't rehearsing in John's basement or riding to the gig together or on stage, we would often be just 'hanging'.

Tom and I would sometimes pick Van up on the way to John's place. I remember the first time very well. Tom drove us to a small, green house behind Mass Ave not far from Central Square. An attractive girl with a fair complexion and long auburn hair answered the door. She looked a little shocked to see us at first, not expecting a short pirate and a sunglass wearing, blues-brother dude at the door, but eventually she let us in.

There was a small baby crawling around on the floor. The only furniture in the place was a rather shoddy-looking green couch with a low coffee table in front of it. A black and white TV stood on a chipped stand in the corner. If Van had any money from his two hit records you couldn't tell from the looks of his apartment. He walked in wearing black pants and a blue ruffled shirt, dressed more for the stage than rehearsal.

"This is my wife, Janet," he said, introducing us. "Why don't you sit down, I'll be right with you."

Janet Planet was a pretty flower child from LA, although at the time I thought she was from Ireland like Van. Janet seemed to be the girl next door type, and like Van, was on the quiet side. She never went to the gigs and rarely came to rehearsals, where she would breastfeed the child while we played. Van seemed to spend much more time with us than he did with his wife, but then he was on a mission.

Tom and I sat on the couch while Van and his wife went into the other room, leaving the baby, Janet's boy, Peter, in our tender care. Apparently they had something to discuss, for we could hear them talking loudly in the next room. The baby, unconcerned at being abandoned by his mother, began to crawl along the couch onto Tom's lap, and proceeded to grab his dark glasses. As Tom was about to object, the kid whacked him on the side of the head with them making Tom jump back. Little Peter, startled as well, lost his balance and fell to the floor, where he landed with a thump on his rump and started squealing.

"What's going on here?" yelled Van, running into the room in alarm. "What did you do to him?"

Tom sat stunned and confused, unable to speak. I was choking with laughter, not able to come to his defense. Van picked up the outraged infant and soothed him with soft words. Janet looked at us from the hallway as if we had just attempted to murder her firstborn child.

Van Morrison was a strange dude. Although he was down to earth and friendly enough, he was hard to really get to know. Even when we hung together he seemed to keep apart, as if an outsider who didn't quite belong. The three of us were about the closest thing to friends he had in Boston, yet he kept his feelings pretty much to himself, except when he sang. He certainly could get riled up, especially when some club owner tried to take advantage of him, but most of the time he was quiet and soft spoken. He definitely wasn't afraid to express his opinion of other performers.

"What do you think of so-and-so?" Tom would ask.

"That faggot!" Van would answer.

"What do you think of *that* band?" John would query of his favorite group.

"Those faggots!" Van would reply.

This response probably had more to do with his growing up in Belfast and Northern Ireland where you had to be macho to survive than with any homophobia on his part, but it certainly could raise eyebrows.

"Who *do* you like?" I finally asked, wondering if there were any other singers he cared for.

"Janis Joplin," he said. "She drinks the same thing I do, Southern Comfort."

We all laughed. Other than John Coltrane, Janis, and Ray Charles, I don't remember him having too many nice things to say about any other performers. I generally agreed with his assessments, but then I was a musical snob.

I don't think Van ever smoked dope. I never saw him take a toke of anything stronger than nicotine. One day after rehearsal Tom and I asked him if he wanted to get high.

"No, man, I can't," he replied. "I burnt out my brain on hash when I was younger and can't handle it any more."

32

I kind of believed him. Perhaps that accounted for his lack of social skills. We were lucky if he said more than two sentences at a time. Or maybe the stuff just made him paranoid.

He certainly wasn't what I'd call articulate, although I've heard him on interviews in recent years talking about Ireland where he sounded downright eloquent. At this time, however, forty-six years ago, he had trouble expressing himself, at least in public situations, and I could well attribute it to something like an overindulgence of one drug or another, although I can swear I never saw Van take any dope of any kind whatsoever. Booze, however, was another story, though it would be awhile yet before we'd see that side of him.

One day Van asked Tom to take him down to State Street to see his lawyer. It was after rehearsal so we all decided to go. We jumped in Tom's car, Van in the front with Tom, John, and I in the back, and headed downtown toward Government Center where Van's lawyer had his office. John was playing air guitar to a rock tune on the radio, while Tom sang the bass lines in his off-key, gravelly voice. I pounded on the upholstery and seatbacks keeping time as usual. It took forever to get through traffic. The car's engine coughed and wheezed to the music like an asthmatic drum machine. Finally, we arrived at the State Street office. Tom pulled into an almost legal spot and we piled out of the car like circus clowns, all dressed in outlandish outfits, our long hair blowing in the wind.

Entering an imposing building through large, brass-handled doors, we found an elevator and pushed the button to the tenth floor. For some reason Tom, who was giddy by nature, got into a laughing jag when John inadvertently passed wind in the elevator. Van looked at them as if asking himself why he had brought them along. I, not a bit amused, tried to pretend I wasn't with them, but it was obvious from my getup that I was part of the show.

We waited in a plush lobby while Van was ushered into a conference room to talk with the big-wig lawyers he had hired to handle his legal hassles with Bang Records. By the looks of it, someone was paying a pretty penny to deal with the thugs who held his record contract.

I never felt so out of place in my life, as if I had stepped out of Toon-Town into the real world. Everyone who walked by did a double-take. Some of the looks we got weren't exactly friendly, but we didn't mind. We were in Van's band, man!

33

Van came out of the meeting visibly agitated and gave us an earful on the way down to the street, stuffing as many f-words into his sparse sentences as possible.

"Those bleeping mother-bleepers are trying to bleep me. Bloody bastards!"

Under a restraining order, he couldn't even approach another record company. If things didn't work out in his favor he'd be playing in the subways in Boston and I'd be right there with him, living beneath a steam vent in the Fens.

As I've said, Van kept his feelings to himself. Maybe it was the result of his recent legal hassles that made him distrustful of people. Perhaps it was because he was a stranger in a strange land. Maybe it was because he thought of himself above it all, the great rock star. He always seemed to be conscious of who he was.

I think he liked hanging out with the guys in the group. Like I said, he didn't really have many friends in town. He seemed to enjoy the simple things. All the time we rehearsed together, I never saw him drink except for an occasional can of beer, certainly nothing like the legendary drinking his later reputation would indicate. But we hadn't started gigging yet.

I had never been in a group that did everything together like this before. There are some bands out there that think you have to live together and think alike to make good music. Most of my career I simply showed up for work with my drums and that was the extent of it. At least half the jobs I had throughout school were one night stands with pick-up bands that would never play together again. I liked it that way. Oh, I'd hang with a few of the guys I worked with over the years, mostly people from school like Tom Kielbania or Harvey Swartz – both of whom I played a lot of chess with - but I'm the kind of person who likes to keep my work and off hours separate. I mean, some bands are hard enough to get through a set with let alone spend your off hours with. Van's band was different.

For some reason we all seemed to hit it off, both personally and musically, almost from the beginning. Maybe it had something to do with Van's laid back style, or perhaps it was because the four of us realized something special was happening. After all, we were playing with a bona-fide rock star with two hit songs under his belt. Van was at a critical point in his life and needed all the support he could get, something he could rely on – like a good band. Perhaps it was just chemistry. Whatever it was, the four of us formed a bond that summer that was special, if surprising. It just seemed to happen on its own. Of course, the daily rehearsal regimen - four, six, sometimes eight hours a day - didn't hurt, nor did the fact that Tom was the only one with a car.

One day we were hanging with Van listening to records. I don't remember what we were listening to, but it might have been *Chicago*. We had a bottle of wine and Van was talking about Belfast and how people there didn't like it when he left, as if he was running away or deserting them. He said someone there was always trying to drag you down, make you belong to one side or the other. I assumed he was talking about the religious strife in Northern Ireland, but he could have been talking about anything, like how some people hate to see one of their own escape the hard streets and succeed. Then again, just like his lyrics, I never knew what Van was talking about half the time. I was in my own little world.

Van's preference for and knowledge of jazz won me over on that very first day. My respect for him as a musician only grew. Even during the rehearsals he'd be totally into the music. On stage he'd close his eyes and sing into the microphone as if it were an instrument, often breaking into a phrase of scat or adlibbing as we stretched out an ending. Yeah, I thought in spite of myself. This cat is cool!

Despite my initial attitude, as time went on, I got more into the whole rock scene. Although I'd hardly heard of him when I first started with the band, the more I talked to other people about it, the more I began to realize what I had fallen into.

What made it even more enjoyable was the fact that Van was so unassuming. He never came on like a prima donna, though we never forgot he was the boss. I don't think he ever doubted himself. He seemed to know what he was about and had a single-minded purpose toward his goal. He was, after all, already famous, but it never went to his head. Maybe he, like me, had come to the big city and been humbled.

Until I read it in an old Rolling Stone publication, I had never heard of the famous incident in Boston that summer when Van was purportedly booed off stage while sitting in with the J. Geils blues band singing *Gloria*. Things like that have a way of bringing a person down to earth, although no one ever booed him off the stage when we played *Gloria* with him.

By this time we had a good assortment of tunes. A few covers, but mostly Van's own songs from previous recordings, with a few that would be on his later albums, ranging from blues and rock, to everything in between, all with his unique and instantly recognizable voice in the lead.

He had been busy working behind the scenes getting things ready. He hired a road crew – two guys - and a manager, and started booking clubs around town. In the meantime, we worked every day to get the band in shape.   We were a tight little group by then and ready to hit the road.

Those first few weeks were almost idyllic. One day we were working on tunes in John's basement, playing Frisbee in the backyard, hanging out in Harvard Square, and the next we were on stage with the man. It was like I had gone to sleep in the lap of obscurity and woken up in the arms of fame.

Chapter 6

The Gig that Almost Wasn't

We played a number of venues that summer from small clubs to concert halls, some out on the Cape and others in downtown Boston. The band worked steady and the money was good, exactly what I was looking for to get me through the summer. What had started out as just another gig was turning out to be more exciting than I expected. We hadn't even hit the stage yet and I was already caught up with the glamour of it. I still wanted to go back to school in the fall, but I was beginning to imagine other possibilities.

Some of those first dates were rough. We never knew what to expect, but most of the time the place would be packed. The more we played, the tighter we got as a group and the more things started to gel.

One of the first jobs we had that summer was out on the Cape, an arena in South Dennis. It was early June. We drove to the gigs in the back of a blue van with the instruments. Van rode in the front with one of the road crew. John, Tom, and I would ride in the back with all the equipment, including my drums. The other roadie would follow in his car.

One of the nicest aspects about working with Van was the road crew. You have no idea what a perk it is for a drummer, with half a dozen cases full of drums and cymbals and hardware, to have someone not only carry it for you, but set it up as well. From the house to the van, from the van to the stage and back, all I had to do was sit down and adjust a few things. It was great, one of the benefits of working with a rock star.

We arrived at the job after a two hour ride, during which Van entertained us with stories of his *Them* days. The place looked like a skating rink that someone had let all the ice out of. It had a rutted concrete floor and walls of corrugated metal. The stage was a monstrosity - large enough for a fifty piece band - stuck in a far, dark corner of the building. The acoustics would prove to be atrocious. The sound would be the least of our worries that day.

While John and one of the roadies were setting up the sound system, four of us, Tom, Steve, the other roadie, Van and I, whiled away the time sitting in one of the cars, just shooting the breeze.

Everyone except me had opened a can of beer. I had just finished half a joint and didn't want to ruin my buzz. We were parked right in front of the building. No one thought much about it. We certainly weren't trying to hide anything.

I'm not sure what we were talking about, but it must have been an interesting topic, because we failed to notice the police officer cautiously approaching the vehicle. There was a tap on the window. We looked up to see one of the Cape's finest staring down at us, his badge flashing in the sun. He motioned for Van to roll down the window.

"What are you boys doing?" he asked, looking at Van. The cop's dark sunglasses shielded his eyes like a Lone Ranger mask.

"Nothing," Van answered, not realizing there was a problem.

"You know it's against the law to sit and drink in a parked car?"

We all sat motionless, as if someone has just frozen us with a blast of Arctic air.

"You want to step out of the vehicle," he said. It wasn't a question.

We slowly piled out of the car.

The place was starting to fill up. Lines of teenyboppers were waiting to get in at the front doors. The cop motioned for us to follow him over to his squad car where another officer, this one with sergeant's stripes, sat waiting.

"Found them drinking beers in that car," said the arresting officer, bucking for his own stripes no doubt. "What should we do with them?"

"It's against the law to drink in a parked car around these parts," announced the sergeant. "Someone should of warned them before they came out here. There's young kids around."

He stepped out of the car and looked us over. At that moment Van's manager came rushing out of the arena accompanied by the concert promoter, who looked like he had just witnessed a five car collision with multiple fatalities. People in the crowd, which was getting larger by the minute, were starting to stare.

"What's going on here? What seems to be the problem?" asked the manager, the guy who had booked the gig.

"We found these boys drinking in the parking lot," the sergeant informed him. "Didn't anyone tell them that's illegal? We're going to have to book them."

"Do you know who this is?" replied the manager pointing to his famous client.

"I don't care if it's the Beatles. Drinking in a parked car's against the law."

"I got a thousand people who bought tickets," announced the terrified promoter. "You just can't cancel the show like that. I'll lose my shirt. Jesus, Phil, it's not like they were smoking dope, for Christ's sake! Why don't you lighten up."

"The law's the law, Dave," replied the sergeant. "Look, we don't want to ruin your show but we have a job to do."

"Well, why don't you come inside my office. We can all talk there, OK?"

The promoter led the way while the two cops herded us in like errant sheep, the old one in front, the young one behind, nipping at our heels like a good shepherd dog.

They hustled us into a corner office. I stood by the office door defiantly.

"You, get in here," the young cop ordered.

I glared back at him.

"No," I said. "I wasn't drinking. I can't drink and play. It makes me sloppy."

I turned to the older cop, the one with all the stripes on his arms - no doubt for busting unwary drinkers in parking lots. He was staring at me with a probing look.

"I wasn't drinking," I repeated, looking him straight in the eye.

"OK, just stay there," he said, believing me.

"But..." objected the younger cop, not wanting to let me off the hook so easily.

"Did you see him drinking, Ernie?"

"Well, no, not really, just the two in the back seat there, and this one." He pointed to Van.

"Well then, he's OK. I believe him. Let him be."

"Yes, sir, sorry, sir," said the rookie, looking at me with a venomous expression and fingering the butt of his revolver like he wanted me to make his day. In spite of my reprieve, I stood rooted to the spot unable to leave the suspense-filled room. I didn't want to desert my comrades or my ride home.

"Now, what are we going to do with them?" asked the sergeant. "They were breaking the law. They admitted they were drinking beer."

"They didn't mean any harm," said Van's manager. "We've never played here before. How were we to know? We certainly did not intend to ignore any laws. Honest, officer, it won't happen again."

"Let's take them downtown and lock them up," suggested the bad cop right on cue.

They had herded Van and the others into the corner of the room. Van stood dejected at the front of the group looking down at the floor, his hands in front of him as if he were already handcuffed. Tom looked like he'd been caught with the Lindbergh baby. Steve's face appeared as if it had been drained of blood. I stood transfixed at the fate of my three friends, wondering what was going to happen next.

"Ah, cut us some slack, Ernie," said the promoter. "They were only relaxing before the job. Why don't you just give them a warning and let them go to work, eh? I'll have to return all the tickets if the show doesn't go on. Then none of us will get paid, including you, Phil." Even though he looked scared, the promoter seemed to have found his courage. Better yet, it appeared that he had struck a nerve.

"What do you three have to say for yourselves?" asked the sergeant looking at the miscreants. Tom's mouth opened but nothing came out. Steve stood there mute, lost in his own silent misery. Van looked up.

"We didn't mean any disrespect," he said. "We didn't know it was a crime to drink beer in a car. We do it all the time back home. We plan to work down here a lot. We have jobs lined up here all summer. What's wrong with that?"

"These people generate a lot of revenue for the community, Phil," added the promoter, gaining the initiative. "I think you've made your point. We'll do a better job of informing folks what the rules are so this doesn't happen again."

"OK, OK, Dave," said the sergeant. "But no one's above the law. I think these boys have learned their lesson well enough." He turned to Van. "Sorry to inconvenience you, but we got college kids coming here by the thousands in the summer. If we let them sit in their cars and drink, well, things would get pretty wild around here real quick. If we let some big-time record artist come by and flaunt the law, how do you suppose we could tell them kids that they can't, when their idols can do it? You get the picture? Maybe you could mention the fact in your act."

"Sure," said the manager, ushering Van and the rest of us out of the room while he had the chance. The promoter rushed out with us, escorting us all the way to the stage and telling us how sorry he was. The arena was mobbed with people, most of them teenaged girls. All I could see from the bandstand was a mass of bobbing heads.

"Boy that was close," said Tom, still shaken.

John and the other roadie asked what happened.

"F-ing a-holes," growled Van as we got up on the bandstand. You could tell he was a little upset, probably afraid they were going to deport him back to Belfast.

"They're all teenyboppers," I said to Tom, adjusting my drum peddle so my short legs could reach it. He was tuning his bass amidst the hiss and noise of the anxious crowd.

"Yeah, what'd you expect?"

I really hadn't known what to expect on our first job, but I hadn't quite anticipated this. I looked out at the sea of eager faces and wondered just what it was they were waiting for. It certainly couldn't have been what they were about to get.

We started off with a long version of *Domino*. All the pent up rage and fury built up from our confrontation with the law came out in a musical paroxysm. The band was alive! We sizzled like cooked bacon. We played our hearts out, especially Van, but then I had never seen him on stage in front of a live audience before.

Closing his eyes and bending over the microphone as if in pain, his voice full of soulful self-expression, Van spurred us on like a team of high strung horses. John played a brilliant solo, bending notes and throwing his body around the stage with abandon, using the feedback like another instrument. Tom and I bounced the rhythm back and forth like a basketball, driving the beat into the floor and making the stage vibrate. It was raging music, like someone had just let us out of a cage.

Hardly waiting for applause, Van started the next tune, singing with a raw-edged emotion that made you want to break a chair. Then he broke into a harp solo that took over where his voice left off. We were doing all of his best songs, as if we were jamming in John's basement instead of in front of a thousand teenaged kids, the crowd almost forgotten.

"Yeah!" I said to myself. "This cat is the real thing!"

The audience didn't know quite what to make of us and the response was mixed. Toward the end of the two hour set Van did *Gloria*, and the crowd applauded with more enthusiasm than they had all afternoon. Never mind the bad acoustics, the band had never sounded so good. There's something about playing to a live audience that transcends every other experience. Then we did *Brown Eyed Girl* and the crowd went wild, the little, half-dressed teenaged girls wiggling their behinds like fantails.

As Steve and Andy tore down the equipment and lugged it to the van, I noticed the two officers who had almost arrested us, Ernie and Phil. They stood leaning against the wide entrance door, which stood open to let out the streaming crowd. I walked up to the older one, the sergeant, and smiled.

"Well, what did you think of the music?" I asked. "How'd you like it?"

"Not bad," replied the cop. "Especially that first song you did. Not bad at all. What was that?"

"A song called *Domino*. I'm sure you'll be hearing more of it," I said, moving on and feeling vindicated.

I walked out into the late afternoon light. There were still kids waiting around, scattered knots of teenaged girls, not one of them over fifteen. The equipment was loaded, while Tom and John waited in the rear of the van. Van was standing in front of the building near a group of pretty girls waiting for his manager to return with the loot. One of the girls, a little brown-eyed beauty with a short skirt and white blouse detached herself from her friends and stood alone not far from him. Van approached her, and bending down, cupped his hand around his mouth and whispered something in her ear.

Her eyes widened in shock and her jaw dropped open as if unhinged. She stiffened and backed away from him as if he were an adder. I'll never forget the look of utter shock on her face. Van, unperturbed, went on his way as if nothing had happened.

I didn't have time to wonder about it, for the manager soon appeared and we were on our way, but it wouldn't be the last time I'd see him whisper into some young girl's ear. I never learned what it was he said, but it always elicited the same response.

I didn't ask about it as we drove back to Cambridge in the back of the van. I was paid my $150 and was a happy camper. We broke open a six pack and made up for the beer we couldn't drink in the parking lot. It had been a successful gig as far as I was concerned, which meant I had played well and gotten paid. In the summer of '68, it didn't get any better than that.

Chapter 7

Hometown Crush

We had a week off from rehearsals and wouldn't be working again until the following weekend when we would do a gig at a well-known rock club in Boston. I decided to head home to see some of my friends, especially my old girl friend, Linda. I hoped to impress her with my newfound fame.

I boarded a Greyhound bus for Plattsburgh, New York. My hometown is less than thirty miles from the Canadian border. If you've ever been to the Burg, especially back in '68, you'd understand my mixture of dread and anticipation at the thought of returning. To me it seemed like the end of the earth Yet I was homesick for the place and my friends the minute I left.

Nice thing about a small town, a little fame goes a long way. I had already notified all my friends and acquaintances that I was playing drums with Van Morrison. Never mind that I had hardly heard of the guy and didn't like his hit songs. He was my ticket to scoring babes and I wasn't going to let this opportunity slip by without going for the big one, my old high school girlfriend. She had turned around and dumped me after a three year intimate relationship as soon as she really started to blossom - I mean *really* started to look good. The story of my life, but I wasn't going to give up without a fight.

I sat with some black dude, who hopped on just before we left and made a point to sit next to me, although there were plenty of other seats. In the dim light, with my dark tanned face, he probably thought I was a 'brother'. Then he started crowding me, pressing me into the side of the bus as we drove out of town. He fell asleep with his head on my shoulder and his shoulder in my ribs. I was too polite to say anything, especially since he was bigger and older than I was, but after awhile I got fed up. I started to push him back, trying to be as obnoxious as possible, at one point brushing dandruff onto his upturned face. I had it bad at the time. He snorted and pulled his head back as if I'd poured acid on him. He'd had enough, and left to find a vacant spot up front where he started talking to the bus driver, who was also a 'brother'.

I stretched out on my newfound space only to be jarred awake a couple hours later as the bus turned into the Plattsburgh depot, nothing more than a deserted garage in the middle of a drizzling, dark, empty street. It was two am in the Burg. It might as well have been Timbuktu.

All the way home, all I could think about was Linda, her tanned skin and slim figure, her silky, long black hair and long-lashed eyes. In my town she was as close as you could come to model-like perfection, and she had been my girl from ninth grade to the end of my junior year when she blossomed from a skinny, all bones little girl into a thing of perfection. I was there every step of the way, but when the time came and better pickings became available she dropped me like a pair of outdated shoes. It was a defining moment in my youth and had a lot to do with my lack of confidence with women. Now I had a plan. I was about to make a comeback.

I called her first thing the next morning, but she had already gone to the beach. It promised to be a hot day in Upstate New York. I didn't have a bathing suit, so I put on a pair of my dad's lame shorts and one of my striped t-shirts, and went to the beach to look for her. I called a couple of the boys, buddies from high school, who were all back in town for the summer on break from college. We played in the high school band together. Nelson and I had been tied for most talented in the class yearbook during our senior year. He beat me out by one vote, that of our friend Dave, another sax player. Those horn players always stick together. We had a running bet about who would be famous first – one became a judge, the other a well-known North Country teacher, director, and musician. I was well on my way to winning the wager, but winning my old flame's heart was more important.

"What's it like playing with Van Morrison?" Dave asked, as he drove us to the beach in his new Mustang. "Hot damn! I always knew one of the boys would make it. I just didn't think it would be Bebo." They laughed and toasted me with bottles of Bud.

The beach is on the northern tip of Lake Champlain, a nice stretch of sand that runs a quarter of a mile along the shore, taking in a campground as well. It's packed with Canadian girls during the summer. On this hot day I was looking for one girl in particular, a dark-skinned, dark-eyed beauty like the one Van had been singing about. Suddenly I knew what that song was about. Finally, a set of lyrics made sense to me. She was my brown eyed girl. I had to show her I wasn't the loser she thought I was.

We stood around the pavilion, three geeks among all the bronzed sunbathers. I hadn't been out in the sun in a bathing suite since my fourteenth birthday, so other than my face, I was as pale as veal. Whatever prompted me to put on shorts - my father's unstylish ones to boot - I'll never know. I spotted her walking down the boardwalk in her most daring bikini followed by a gaggle of tall, well-tanned, good-looking guys.

I had forgotten how beautiful she was, how much her figure had filled out, how narrow her waist was, how soft her skin. Her long black hair looked like it was made of Ahimsa silk. It shimmered in the light as she moved. The banter of my friends disappeared in a haze of desire. I could hardly move let alone approach her. I stood there like a cigar store Indian while she walked by without even noticing me, although I was pretty hard to miss in my out of style pants and garish t-shirt, like something marooned from a cruise ship.

"Are you going to talk to her or not?" asked Dave, needling me as usual.

"Yeah, you're a big rock star now. Put on the moves, boy," said Nelson. "Now's your chance, look, she's ditched the guys. She's coming back this way."

Nelson was right. Linda had gotten rid of the pack of laughing hyenas and was coming back in my direction, obviously on her way upstream to capture more happy salmon. As she approached, I ditched my buddies, who continued to call after me with wisecracks, and moved to meet her. She had stopped by a railing and stood looking out at the sparkling lake.

"Hi, Linda," I said, coming up behind her. "I thought I recognized you. How you been?"

"Oh, hi, Joey," she replied, turning around and looking at me. I could tell she tried not to look at my hairy, white legs, but her eyes went up and down me like laser beams, taking it all in. She smiled in that condescending way she had that made me feel like a jerk asking for an autograph.

"I'm working with Van Morrison," I blurted out, not waiting for her to ask me what I was doing as I had planned. Her smile grew even more patronizing.

"That's nice. I think I've heard of him."

"*Gloria, Browned Eyed Girl*," I said, dropping names. All of a sudden these were my favorite songs.

"I know that one. I like it. You're working with that guy?"

45

"Yeah, Van and me are good friends. We play it all the time. You've gotta come down to Boston and hear the band sometime. I'll get you in. Find you a place to stay."

"Yeah, sounds like fun," she replied, smiling brightly. Bingo! Finally something was coming my way. Me who had never won a thing in my life had finally hit the jackpot. The luscious thing in the tiny black bathing suit wiggled and pranced before me. She smiled at me, this time no longer mocking but inviting. I could have fallen into her dark, almond eyes. Then I realized that she wasn't smiling at me, but at someone behind me. The gaggle of boys had returned. The tallest and handsomest of them looked down on me as if I were an undersized circus clown.

"Billy, Joey's going to get us tickets to see Van Morrison down in Boston. You know, the one who did *Brown Eyed Girl*."

"Great, you got a date, big guy," he said, as they crowded me out of the way and swept Linda off again to parade her down the boardwalk. My friends had all found their respective mates and had wandered off to do their own thing. I was left alone and broken-hearted, rejected once again. Not even being almost famous could get me any action.

Things weren't much better when I returned home that evening.

"Why didn't you ask before you borrowed my shorts?" my dad said from the kitchen table when I walked in. I hadn't seen him since I'd been home. My mom, who I had spent the early morning talking to, was out with her sister, and my siblings were out with their friends.

"I needed something for the beach. You weren't around so I borrowed them. Couldn't you get something more stylish than this? I was a laughing stock."

"I was playing golf this morning. I was going to ask you to come along, but you were out like a light."

"Yeah, got in late last night. I'm glad I didn't wake you."

"So what's with this Van Morrison Band? Is it a real job? Are you going to be able to support yourself at school next year? Maybe you should get a real job now that we aren't able to help you any longer."

As usual with my dad, he hammered me with so many questions and concerns I felt I'd just been pummeled by Floyd Mayweather. I thought I'd give him a few counter-punches as well.

"This is a real job, Dad," I replied. "We even get paid for rehearsals. Van's got us booked all summer. I'll have money saved by the time school starts. Anyway, I may stay with Van."

"What? What about school?"

"What about it?"

"Well, do you think he's going to stay around Boston? He's a big recording star. He'll be taking off to New York or LA once he's got his legal hassles taken care of."

Dad seemed to know a lot about Van, maybe even more than I did. I hadn't thought about whether or how long Van would be staying in Boston. I decided to keep throwing curves at the old man, to keep him off balance.

"We'll see what happens. For now it's a good gig. I should be able to get plenty of work next year. I have a good reputation. I know a couple agents who can keep me gigging pretty steady. My roommate and I can start a band if it comes to that. Don't worry. Since you brought it up, I'm thinking of changing my major next year, if I stay in school."

"What, from Music Education? I thought we agreed that if you went to Berklee you'd get a degree."

"I can still get a degree, just not teaching kids how to play music."

"What's wrong with that?"

"Nothing, it's just not for me. I don't want to spend my time in a classroom teaching. I've never taught and have no aptitude or interest in it. If I'm going to be working and supporting myself through school I should at least get to say what I'll be studying. If I stay in education I'll have to take student-teaching and other non-music courses. If I switch to arranging and composition, I'll learn how to write and arrange music, like Quincy Jones. I could write for the movies or TV shows, or teach music at a higher level. Maybe I'll follow up at Julliard or Eastman and get my masters."

I knew dropping the names of two prestigious New York music schools would grab his imagination.

"Oh, you know who I saw the other day?" he said, changing the subject on a dime as he usually did when I got the upper hand.

"No, who?" I asked, glad for a new topic.

"Your little girlfriend there, that Kimble girl."

"First of all she's not little anymore, and secondly, she hasn't been my girlfriend for over a year now."

"Well, I told you she was going to be a beauty. All skin and bone, boy did she fill out nice. She always smiles and says hi."

Without even trying Dad had thrown me into a major funk. That's all I needed, my old man telling me how gorgeous my ex-girlfriend was. What's she doing smiling at him, anyway?

"That's nice," I replied.

Now that he had totally ruined my day, my lower Scorpio nature took over. I wasn't going to leave without shaking his cage.

"Anyway, if Van goes to New York and LA, I may go with him, who knows."

"What about school? You just said you wanted to get your masters."

"It all depends. We'll see. I can always go back to school later. Who knows, maybe I'll go right by Berklee."

"This opportunity won't come along again. I've got all I can do to send you to college as it is. We've been going without and saving for the past twenty years, damn it!"

"Calm down, Dad. You don't have to yell."

"Well let me make myself perfectly clear. If you drop out of school, that's it. I won't be able to pay your way. It will be your brother's turn. If you want to go back you'll have to do it on your own. You better think twice before you throw your life away."

"That's the whole point, Dad. It's my life. I'm not going to throw anything away. I appreciate what you're doing. I'm just saying playing with Van is a big opportunity too and I want to keep my options open."

My brother Jim came in soon after and we went off to see another old friend, Jerry Levene, who was playing solo guitar at the local Holiday Inn, the highpoint of my visit, but I didn't get much sleep that night. As I lay awake wondering what the future would bring, the conversation with my father repeating in my head, images of Linda in her black bikini fought against my brother's snoring to drive sleep away like a barking dog a flock of geese.

I returned to Boston the next day thoroughly depressed. My big dream of renewing my relationship with Linda had been dashed on the hard rocks of reality. She was out of my league, Van Morrison or no Van Morrison. I knew the conversation with my father hadn't ended and I was skating on thin ice where his patience was concerned. Little did I know I was headed for a piece of music history.

Chapter 8

The Mad Tea Party

The weekend after my Plattsburgh trip, Van had us booked at the Boston Tea Party. Finally, we were playing a legitimate club instead of some skating arena in the middle of scrub pines. In a way, this was our debut in Boston. We were all excited.

The Tea Party was on 53 Berklee Street in the South End at the time. It was one of the better known clubs in town where bands like Led Zeppelin and Cream played when they came to the Hub. It was a high-ceilinged room filled with psychedelic lights, which sprayed the walls with moving colors. I'd been to the place once or twice to try and pick up girls, but it was always too loud to make conversation and I didn't dance, so I never got very far. Now I was here with the main attraction.

The place was packed with flower-children and hippy wannabes. The crowd was generally receptive. Van put on a memorable performance and everyone played well, although I was having trouble that night. The acoustics were good, but we were playing hard, as loud as we could. My right foot was kicking my bass drum like a rawhide punching bag, but it kept sliding away from me because the pegs I used to hold it were not working on the slippery, hardwood floor. Every so often I had to grab it and pull it back into place, which didn't help my concentration or the beat.

To make matters worse, I had decided to wear my Sgt. Pepper's jacket, a heavy purple thing with gold thread running through it in flowered patterns, replete with epaulettes on the shoulders. I must have looked like a real idiot, but I thought it was cool. I don't know what possessed me to change from my usual striped t-shirts and bellbottoms to this piece of costume nonsense. No doubt in my misplaced sense of style I thought it would help me with the babes. As it turned out it had the opposite effect.

It was the most impractical getup I could have contrived, binding and hot and altogether difficult to play in. I started sweating profusely after the second song and was soaking wet by the end of the third. It dripped down my eyebrows and into my eyes. It dropped from the end of my nose onto the head of my snare. It dribbled from my mustache and ears. If someone could have rung me out I would have started a waterfall over the bandstand. I was drenched.

Instead of picking up girls as had been my original intent during the breaks, I spent the time between sets drying myself with paper towels, which I used up like a ninety-year-old with hay fever. Of course my jacket held the wetness like a sponge, so when I put it back on it was just as wet as when I had taken it off, all the drying and wiping in vain.

The second set went well in spite of my discomfort. I managed to hold things together as Van counted off the tempos a little faster than usual, and dynamics were thrown out the window. Everyone had turned up their amps to maximum volume. My drums were never mic'd, so I could hardly make myself heard over the din even though I had my largest sticks and was pounding the drum heads as hard as I could, splashing cymbals like I was mad at them. There was a lot of energy and spontaneity on the bandstand that night and it seemed to catch on, as the enthusiasm of the crowd appeared to increase by the end of the second set.

Oh, did I mention, Van was pretty much plastered out of his gourd? This was the first time we had really seen him drink. He hadn't had much chance at the last job on the Cape, and this was a bona-fide rock club where that sort of thing was condoned if not promoted.

Like his first outburst of temper, which we had yet to witness, his first drinking bout took us all by surprise. While the instruments were being set up and tuned, and everything readied on stage, Van sequestered himself in the small dressing room we had and downed a pint of Southern Comfort. I know this because when I left him the bottle was full and when I returned ten minutes later to get my towel, it was two-thirds empty. Just the thought of it made me tipsy. I wondered how he could drink that much whiskey so fast and not be comatose.

I didn't know what to expect, but other than adding a bit more passion to his performance, it had small effect. If anything it seemed to enhance it. There was a bit more edge in his already edgy voice, a little more jerk to his spastic movements. He held the mike with both hands and sang into it with all the anguish and pain a poor Belfast boy could muster; his face screwed-up and contorted as if he were having sex. He scatted and improvised lyrics, and played long, soulful solos on the harp, putting on a raw, energetic performance that seemed to please the crowd.

Sometimes he would chug a few down between sets, sometimes on the way home in the back of the van. No matter where or how much he never seemed intoxicated. I never saw him stagger or heard him slur his words. Outside of the gig I never saw him drink more than a can of beer. On stage, however, or at a concert, he was invariably looped.

To my embarrassment we ended the night with *Gloria* and *Brown Eyed Girl*. The flower-children and hippies looked at us like we had just landed in a cup and saucer, although they clapped politely at the end as if their parents had just finished playing. To me they were the worst tunes to play in a club like the Tea Party, but then these were his big hits, the reason he probably got the gig in the first place. So I swallowed my pride and played them down as loud and fast as I could. The contrary reaction of the South Denis crowd and this audience to the same songs was striking, though it made sense to me since I felt much the same. It must have made an impression on Van as well, and caused him to wonder just where he was headed at this crossroad in his life.

The next day there was a review in the paper. It was our first write-up in the local press, the first in my career. It wasn't bad, although I never knew quite what to make of these things, and really don't remember much about what it said.

I recall the writer commented on Van's strong voice and unique singing style, which he labeled as blues rock with some African rhythms thrown in, whatever that meant. I took it as a compliment, although it was obvious to me they didn't know quite what to make of us. I can't say I blamed them. As I said, we were a curious mixture of opposing styles. Van didn't seem altogether unpleased with the review, but he was never totally happy with what anyone wrote about him.

"Bloody a-hole!" he exclaimed, after reading it.

The Tea Party was the first place we saw local celebrities, like Peter Wolf from WBCN, come back stage to see Van. They'd usually bring a bottle of Scotch whiskey and ask him insipid questions about other bands and musicians.

"You sound like Mick Jagger," Peter observed, obviously trying to give Van a complement. Van responded with his usual two word response. The startled look on their faces was priceless. Unfortunately no one ever told him he sounded like Ray Charles. He would have taken *that* as a compliment.

Van kept business matters to himself. He seldom volunteered much information and we never asked. I'm not sure what deal he had with the other guys. I assumed it was the same as mine. No matter what happened at the door and what his take was, Van always paid me the agreed $150, whether he made any money or not. I got paid the same each week for rehearsals and for each gig, and Van worked every weekend at a minimum.

Things were good. What started out as a dismal summer with the alarming prospect of being cut off and having to support myself or drop out of school, turned out to be the best summer of my life. I was working steady at a good paying job that would not only allow me to save money, but increase my prospects of future work. Nothing like two months with the Van Morrison band on a drummer's resume, even if he was a jazz drummer.

Chapter 9

Blowup at the Supermarket

The more I think back on that time, the more I appreciate Van's good nature and generally easy going attitude. He never once became uptight with any of us in the band. When he got riled up, however, it was something to behold. He became a completely different person, like Jekyll and Hyde, quiet one minute, a raving maniac the next.

I'll never forget the first time I saw Van blow up. We were playing the Psychedelic Supermarket on the upper end of Commonwealth Ave. It was somewhat like the Boston Tea Party but not as well known, though it showcased a lot of the same bands. We were looking forward to playing there even though it was a middle of the week gig. It was exciting to be on the same stage that some of the more progressive and famous rock bands had played.

We arrived at the back of the building and started to unload the equipment. Van had joined us in the van for the short ride from Cambridge. Cars whizzed by on the Mass Turnpike, which was just across the street from the club. Whatever our expectations might have been that night, we were sorely disappointed the moment we entered the ugly, square concrete building.

It was cold and dark, like an unused hanger, not at all inviting like the Tea Party had been, with few lights and those just one step above bare bulbs. And unlike the Tea Party, this place was empty, as dead as a tomb. Even after we had set up and tuned our instruments and were ready to play, it was still devoid of a single customer.

Van waited twenty minutes until four or five single guys wandered in - more to get out of the rain than to see the band - before he started the first set. It was the longest set I ever remember playing, like being in the outfield while the other team bats around the order again and again until the game is called on account of darkness. I never hated *Brown Eyed Girl* more in my life. *Gloria* seemed to go on forever, finally emptying the place of its last two patrons. We were lucky if ten people showed up all night.

To make matters worse, the room had a hollow, empty sound that we just couldn't seem to fill up. Perhaps the lack of people had something to do with it. Maybe it was our measly little amplifiers. The dampness of the curtains behind the stage made my drums sound like dead raccoon skins. My sticks had as much bounce as two lead weights in the damp atmosphere. This was one of the few times I remember Van performing with his back to the audience, which he did practically the entire night, although there were few people there to snub. Then the fun began.

It was our last set. Our break had already gone fifteen minutes past our normal time and Van still hadn't called us back up to the stage. I was wondering if we were going to play or not, when the club owner came up, a short, dark man in a crumpled suit whose name turned out to be George Papadopoulos. He spoke with a thick accent, which was only made worse by his agitation.

"Why are you not going on?" he demanded.

"Because there's nobody here," answered Van. "You told me there would be a good crowd."

"I never guaranteed nothing," said the man, defensively. "I said that we've had good Thursday night crowds in the past. It depends on the band."

"There's a game tonight," volunteered Tom. "I wonder if that has anything to do with it." Fenway was only a few blocks away. Everyone ignored him.

"When I agreed to play here," said Van, getting mad, "you f-ing told me there would be at least a hundred people. I'm not playing for a percent of the door if there're no f-ing people. We had a guaranteed minimum."

"We had no guarantees," said the little man vehemently. "How can I tell how many people will show up? It's still early, but they no come if you not play." It was after eleven, a peak time.

Van exploded, packing as many f-words as he could into the next few short sentences, swearing like a Revere Beach gangster at the top of his lungs. The rest of us stood there in shock. I had never heard such an outburst at that point in my life, and could hardly believe it was coming from the mild-mannered person I had come to know. He was so flustered he got momentarily tongue-tied and was unable to speak.

This was when I first learned that Van was playing for a piece of the door, and became worried for my own supper. As I've said, Van kept the business matters to himself. So none of us knew what was going on, except that we had always gotten paid in the past. I hoped that wasn't about to change.

Van got his second wind and went off on another swearing tirade when the club owner tried to argue his case, yelling as loud as he could in a thick Irish accent. The two of them sounded like the UN on a bad day. I thought for a moment Van was going to pop the guy, and found the whole thing very amusing, but then I was a warped kid. Eventually a compromise was reached and we ended up doing the last set.

This one was the worst of the whole disastrous evening. Van, ripped on Southern Comfort by this time and in a foul mood, with his back to the small audience that had finally started to arrive, turned it into a stressful rehearsal, stopping us in the middle of the songs and changing the tempos halfway through the choruses. It was as if we couldn't do a single thing right. I mean, it wasn't our fault nobody turned up that night, but it sure felt like it.

I'm not sure what the final deal was between Van and the club owner, but we were paid as usual. That was one of the best things about working with the guy, no matter what happened I got paid the agreed upon amount.

I was surprised when I saw that my friend Louie Peterson had stopped by. I hadn't notice him come in, but he was standing by the stage when I walked down the steps.

"Hey, Bebo, how's it going?"

"Hi, Louie, what brings you out tonight?"

"Rehearsing for Charlie's album, the studio's not far from here. Saw you guys were playing. Thought I'd drop by. Hey, what's with Van? Is he always like that?"

"Naw, we're having a bad night. I think he's miffed at the small door. You should have heard him and Papadopoulos go at it."

Hearing Louie go on about Mariano and all the good players he was working with didn't do much for my mood, which like my playing that night was sour. It wouldn't have been so bad if I had played well, but I just couldn't seem to get anything working, not that Van gave us half a chance. Of all nights for Louie to show up!

Things were rather quiet during the short ride back to John's house where we kept the equipment. I envied Louie, and wished I had gotten the Charlie Mariano gig. A few more nights like this and I'd have to start drinking myself.

Although I admired this intense, little Irishman more each day – even more so after his tantrum - Van's type of music certainly wasn't doing my jazz chops any good, as I reminded myself for the twentieth time that summer. Then again, Charlie Mariano didn't have roadies.

Chapter 10

The Roadie's Girl

Working with a rock star has its benefits. One, as I've mentioned, is the road crew, who carried our equipment and set it up on stage. One of the guys, Steve, not only carried all my drums, he actually could piece them together, which is really an art because every drummer is different. From the slant of the snare and small-tom, to the layout of the various cymbals, Steve seemed to know just how I liked them. All I had to do was jump on stage, sit down, and adjust a few things. I got to know him fairly well.

He was a tall, lanky, good-looking kid with curly blond hair, a nice, down home American boy. He looked like he should have been the rock star. Instead, he was carrying drums and amplifiers for the band.

I'm sure Steve would have traded his good looks to sit behind the drums and play with Van. He practically worshipped the guy. When he got drunk, he would gush how much he loved music, but couldn't play a note or keep a beat. Steve was another one of those Jekyll and Hyde characters, calm and friendly one minute, homicidal the next. Of course, he had a good reason to be crazy - he had a beautiful girlfriend.

Beverly was a perfect, petite ten with braided black hair and dark eyes, and a body that wouldn't quit, which she liked to show off. As beautiful as my old girlfriend back home was, Linda was a poor man's version of Steve's girl. I first met her when Steve invited me over for dinner one evening. We came in to find Beverly on the couch with another guy, sitting way too close for comfort. Steve immediately blew up and wanted to know what the hell was going on. So did I!

"We're just watching a movie," said the dark-eyed beauty. "We weren't doing anything."

"What's he doing here?" yelled Steve, as if he hadn't heard her.

Yeah, I said to myself, eyeing her suspiciously. What's that guy doing here?

"Steve," she pouted. "Don't be like that."

"Get out," he yelled at the guy, threateningly. "I don't want you here when I'm not around!"

About time I thought, jealously. *We don't want you around here even when Steve is here!*

I couldn't take my eyes off her, as the embarrassed and intimidated visitor mumbled his apology and headed for the door. I wished it had been me sitting there all tangled on the couch with her, even if it would have meant probably getting shot.

Though I couldn't blame Steve for being riled, I was surprised at his outburst and violent temper. He had always seemed like such a calm, peaceful person. Then again, a beautiful woman has a way of doing that to a guy. I should know.

The rest of the evening was quiet enough, though I had trouble concentrating on dinner. I could understand Steve's jealously, but didn't think it fair. The roadies were practically the only ones who scored with the groupies. Van would attract them, but these two tall, good-looking guys caught them. I'd seen Steve hook up enough times to think his outburst a bit disingenuous, if not unjustified. I mean, how could a guy cheat on a to-die-for girl like Beverly?

Of course, all they talked about was Van. What's it like to play with him? Who does he admire? Does he do drugs? What's he really like? Even though Steve worked for him, he was just as star struck as the teenyboppers who crowded the dance floors of the arenas we played.

I didn't care much for their record collection, which they played for me after dinner, nor their musical tastes, but I would have sat listening to the Rolling Stones and Cream all night to be with Steve's dark-eyed beauty. The evening ended nice enough. Steve and his girl stood in the doorway of their flat to say bye; Steve behind, saying he'd see me for the gig the next day; Beverly in front, looking provocatively at me with an inviting smile. I didn't want to leave and thought about her all night. Little did I know I would soon be experiencing Steve's jealousy firsthand.

The next day we were playing somewhere on the Cape, another arena full of teenaged girls. As usual, I rode in the back of the van with the others, while Steve drove to the job in his hot little, red sports car with Beverly. He didn't normally take her along. Perhaps he didn't want to leave her alone after the previous evening. After the gig, we all went to get a bite to eat at a local car-hop joint.

Much to my pleasant surprise, Beverly invited me to join them. There were only two seats in Steve's small sports coup, but this was ten times better than sitting in the back of the van with Tom and John.

Van was driving with his manager. Hardly believing my good fortune, I jumped in the bucket seat without a second thought. Beverly proceeded to sit on my lap.

She was exuberant and vivacious as ever, bouncing up and down on my thigh as we drove to the restaurant, talking non-stop. She was excited about being with the band. I'm sure she would have preferred sitting on Van's lap, but as far as I could tell she didn't seem to mind whose lap she was sitting on.

As we drove, she talked about her favorite bands and singers.

"I just love Bob Dylan," she said at one point.

My bubble burst then and there. Beautiful or not, I just had to comment on her lack of taste.

"Bob Dylan!" I said. "How can you listen to him? That guy's got the worst voice I've ever heard. His group sounds like a jug band."

"But his lyrics are so poetic and deep," she countered earnestly.

"How can you even understand what he's saying? He mumbles his words. He sings out of key. I can't even listen to him long enough to know what he's singing about."

"How can you say that?" she said, her lips pouting. She sounded hurt. I was instantly sorry for my outburst.

"Van's lyrics are like Dylan's in a lot of ways," said Steve, "especially some of his newer songs."

I felt like saying, what do you know, but refrained when I realized he was probably right. After all, I didn't have a clue what Van's lyrics were about. As great as Bob Dylan obviously is, I never liked any of his drummers at the time. As I've said, I just couldn't get by that.

"Yeah, I guess so," I conceded. "But Van's ten times a better singer." I still wanted to make my point, like a politician who just can't seem to shut up. "Van's got a great voice, real unique and bluesy. He knows how to use it and project it. He's got a great ear and good control. The cat knows what he's doing."

"So does Dylan," said Beverly, squirming on my knee.

Steve didn't seem to mind Beverly sitting on my lap at first. Then I noticed him down-shifting a little more violently and taking the corners a bit faster. He kept looking at us out of the corner of his eye as we sat there having a good time. I was concentrating so hard on Beverly I hardly noticed when we just missed a street sign, as he jerked the car toward the side of the road.

Suddenly, Steve picked up the coke can sitting next to him and whipped it out the passenger side window, just missing my nose by an inch. I saw it bouncing down the road behind us out of the rearview mirror, spraying soda-suds.

Beverly stopped talking and looked at Steve nervously. I stared straight ahead. No one said a word until we stopped at the take-out stand. Then Steve asked us what we wanted as if nothing had happened, and was as pleasant as could be as we ate our burgers and fries. Beverly sat rigid on my thigh as if she couldn't stand the touch of me, while I expected a plastic fork in the juggler any minute. Needless to say, I rode home in the back of the van with Tom and John that night.

Steve continued to set up my kit at the gigs, but he never invited me to his apartment again. I saw Beverly once more toward the end of the summer when one of Van's backers threw a party for him, but she was too busy flirting with the rich guys to even acknowledge me. That didn't faze me, though. My moment of fame had only just begun.

Chapter 11

Cuts Like a Knife

Playing with one another and hanging together, I got to know Tom and John pretty well, but everyone has secrets, a dark side best kept hidden. At that time, Tom was one of my best friends. Even before Van we hung together, playing chess in the park and jamming.

He may not have looked like a rock star, but Tom had a heart of gold. As I've said, he's one of the nicest guys you'd ever want to meet. Sometimes that will get you further in life than good looks.

One day during the summer, while we were working with Van, Tom and I double dated. We had to drive out to Springfield, Mass to meet the girls. I didn't know who his date was, but she had a friend. Tom raved about this girl all the way out, but I wondered how pretty she could be. I mean, I loved Tom, but he, like me, wasn't that successful with women and never seemed to care about his appearance.

I didn't know what to expect, but expected the worst. I was pleasantly surprised. My date didn't look half bad, though her father, who kept circling the theater in his pickup, was a drag.

Tom's girl was downright cute. She seemed to be very attentive, but I was afraid for my friend. I knew how much he liked her and only saw trouble for him. She was a heartbreaker for sure and poor Tom wore his heart on his sleeve.

On the way home I tried to warn him.

"She's going to break your heart," I said, me the wise one on the ways of the world, who hadn't had a date in three years.

"Naw," he replied. "She's not like that. I'm going to marry her."

Poor Tom, I thought. She's going to make him miserable.

"Well, I hope I'm around to pick up the pieces," I warned.

Her name was Claudette, and Tom did end up marrying her. They had four wonderful children together and ten granchildren. Shows you what I know.

I can't say I ever really hung around with John, just him and me. As I've said, he was just a kid, a whole three years younger than I, but I did get to know his dark side.

We were playing yet another Cape Cod gig. The place, a white wooden structure, looked like a church with its steep roof and steeple.

Inside was a small hall, with a stage at one end and rows of long, wooden benches, which had been moved back to make room in front of the bandstand for people to gather.

The acoustics were atrocious. It was like playing in a barn. The band sounded bad that night and Van seemed to be more tanked than usual. John was playing particularly loud and raucous, with a lot of out of tune cords and feedback. Halfway through the first set, he started smashing my cymbals with the neck of his guitar. Tom and I looked at each other in surprise.

Tom knew how mad I got when someone hit my cymbals. He'd seen me rap the knuckles of more than one drunk with my drumsticks when they'd get cute and start hitting my cymbals while I was playing. It didn't matter how big they were. Size 2b sticks are like clubs. I glared hard at John. It only seemed to make him crazier. Now he was smashing them on every beat, almost knocking my crash cymbal over.

I figured it was something he'd seen one of his rock idols do, maybe Pete Townsend of the *Who*, but it was really getting on my nerves. I kept playing, but by now the beat was nowhere to be found amid the wild noise of guitar chords and crashing cymbals. When the set ended, as soon as we were backstage, I confronted him angrily. I never wanted to smack anybody more in my life.

"What's the big idea, John? What do you think you're doing?"

"I don't know," he replied. "I guess I got carried away."

"Well, if you hit my cymbals again, they'll have to carry *you* away!"

Van had disappeared into the closet-sized dressing room for a second round of Southern Comfort. He couldn't have cared less if John had lit my drums on fire.

The very first song of the next set, John started smashing my cymbals again with his guitar. I glared at him as if he had just castrated my prize bull. It was hard enough to play in this place with its two-bit sound system and lousy acoustics. Not only could I not hear, but my drums kept creeping away from me across the slippery, hardwood floor. Soon they were scattered in four different directions halfway across the stage. I had to stretch my legs and arms to try to reach them, and constantly had to pull them in so I could play[2].

Finally, John hit one of my cymbals so hard it crashed to the floor and went splashing off the stage. Even Van looked around in surprise.

---

[2] I hadn't yet learned the trick of using a carpet, and the chain and nail I had to keep things together were practically useless.

The audience thought it was part of the act. By the end of the set I was ready to brain the kid.

I never got the chance. When I finally tracked him down he was cutting his arm, which was covered with a series of small scars, with a pocket knife.

"What's with you?" I asked. "What are you, nuts?"

"Yeah," he said. "I want to hurt myself. Hit me! Beat me up!"

I don't know, maybe he didn't get his thorazine that night, but he was really messed up. Of course, I no longer wanted to punch him out. I just wanted to get away from him.

"OK, John, cool it," I said. "Your crazy act worked. Forget it. Just don't cut yourself anymore."

It was another loud, long night, with plenty of missed beats and bungled chord changes, Van drunk out of his mind. Yet, for some reason, the crowd seemed to like it all the same.

"You guys sounded great," some guy said to me after the show.

"I'll be the judge of that," I retorted rudely, offended at being complimented when I knew we must have sucked. But then I always was a musical snob, as if I was the only one with any kind of taste. I couldn't have cared less what the crowd thought. As it turns out, they were probably right. It was Van they were clapping for, not the band. You can't argue with a room full of applauding people, no matter how smart you think you are.

You never know, good luck, bad, sometimes you can't tell. What I thought was the worst night I'd yet had playing with Van turned out to be the evening of my dreams.

Chapter 12

Love and Rejection

Obviously, almost all the groupies who showed up at our gigs wanted Van. The band would get his cast-off's, which were about 99.99 percent of them. I mean other than whispering into a young girl's ear once in awhile, he was practically a monk.

It's hard to hook up with someone when you all drive to the gig together in the back of a van. I'm not aware of anyone in the band, except maybe one of the good-looking roadies, ever getting lucky at a gig. We just weren't that kind of band and in many of the places we played you'd be lucky if there was a girl there over sixteen.

I didn't have a girlfriend at the time. Heck, I was lucky if I could even meet a girl. I was in a three year funk and hadn't had a real date since my senior year in high school, partly due to a lack of funds, and partly because of my complete lack of social skills. I could barely carry on a decent conversation with someone of the opposite sex. So like the others, I usually went home alone.

Still, it's hard not to meet women when you're playing in a band with Van Morrison. At this time in my life, you'd have to be an absolutely predatory female if you wanted to get me in bed. I had no come-on and even less confidence. How I came to be this way is a long, sad story. Suffice it to say I was in a major slump. Playing drums with Van Morrison almost changed that.

We were staying over at the Cape that night, since we had another gig lined up for the next day. I dreaded spending the night in a room with John after what had happened. The mere thought gave me the heebie-jeebies. I mean, what if he decided to cut me? Fortunately, as it turned out, I didn't have to worry.

As I walked to the front of the stage after the job, I noticed there was still quite a crowd milling about, most of them girls wanting to talk to Van, but older chicks, not the usual teenyboppers, who were all home in bed by this time. This crowd was older and hipper. As Van could only handle four or five at a time, and with the roadies working and John busy cutting himself, I got lucky.

She was a cute blonde with a deep bronze tan and perfect butterball body. Her short curly hair and fresh pretty face instantly attracted me. Her bright blue eyes looked me over as I approached her, hurriedly trying to think of something to say. I don't know, maybe because I was mad at John and didn't give a damn, I wasn't as nervous as usual. I walked right up to her and asked her how she liked the concert.

"Great," she said. "I just love the drums."

"Yeah, me too," I said lamely. "What's your name?"

"Ann," she said.

"Hi, Ann, I'm Joe."

With my meager repertoire of phrases exhausted, I was soon plunged into embarrassing silence. I needn't have worried. Ann talked enough for both of us. She was just full of questions, like a reporter on a hot scoop. She asked questions about Van and about the group, and where I went to school and where I grew up. She quizzed me on my favorite band and what I liked to eat for breakfast. She asked me what TV shows I watched and what books I read, and if I liked sports or not. She seemed possessed with finding out everything there was to know about me in as short a time as possible. Even better, she asked me if I'd like to come back to her place.

She had a cabin on the beach, a gray-shingled job with a cozy pine interior. We didn't waste much time talking after that. Before I knew it our lips were locked and we were groping each other like grooming monkeys.

Thank God for predatory females!

We drank some wine. In the glimmering candle-lit room, with her golden blonde hair and bronze velvet skin, she was the most beautiful thing I had ever seen. I almost fell into her deep blue eyes. Her mouth was as soft as a petal. She was exquisite and obviously way too good for me. But the longer it took her to find that out the better it was for yours truly.

I was totally inept as usual, but Ann, though only twenty-one, was a woman of experience, and seemed more than satisfied with the encounter. Oh, to be young again!

The next day was drizzling and damp. We slept late and had a leisurely breakfast, as Ann continued to pepper me with questions. I lied to the best of my ability, pretending to be cultured and politically correct. I had to rehearse with the band that afternoon. She promised to come to the gig that night and drove me back to the motel where Van and the others were staying. The guys grilled me on my evening, but I was tired of answering questions and never was one to kiss and tell – until now that is.

As promised, Ann was there later that evening, standing in the first row in front of the bandstand. John must have gotten his medication, because he didn't once smash any of my cymbals with his guitar. After the gig I introduced Ann to Van and asked if she could come back to Boston with us. He said it was fine with him, and when we drove home that night, Ann was with us in the back of the van.

Van was quite talkative and seemed to be in a good mood, passing the bottle around and telling stories about his days in Ireland and LA, who he liked and who he didn't, dropping names like Mick Jagger and Jim Morrison as if he had grown up with them. I wasn't sure I liked the way Ann was looking at him, with this kind of adoring reverence. I wondered if she had just been using me to get to him, not that she couldn't have used me any way she wanted. That girl owned me body and soul after the first five minutes in that cabin.

When we stopped at my place Ann seemed a bit reluctant to get out of the van, and sat there talking to my boss as if she expected him to close the door and whisk her away. Little did she know, lucky for me, he had a new wife to go home to. Finally, Ann got out and the van drove away, leaving us standing alone under the street lights in the early morning dark.

At that time I lived in a three-story stone building on Gloucester Street, above an insurance agency. The place was situated between Mass Avenue and Commonwealth, in the shadow of the towering Prudential building, the tallest structure in the city at the time. My roommate was staying at his girlfriend's, so I had the apartment to myself. I opened the glass-paneled door to the building and led her up the stairs to my second floor, one-bedroom flat.

On entering, I opened a large window overlooking the street and let some air into the stuffy apartment. Then I hurriedly ran around the room picking up loose clothes from where I had thrown them before getting ready for the weekend job at the Cape. Moving a pile of dirty dishes from the sink, I washed two glasses so we could drink some of the wine she had brought. The sounds of the late night city filtered into the room from the open window. I lit a candle to create some atmosphere and put some jazz on the stereo. Things went downhill from there.

She wasn't thrilled with my musical selection and when she went to look for something better became even more annoyed.

"You don't have one rock album here. I thought you said you liked rock?"

"Yeah, some of it," I admitted. "I don't buy the stuff. My roommate has some things you might like, but he took most of his records to his girl's house. I think there's a Beatles album in there somewhere."

"How about some Stones?" she suggested.

"The Stones suck," I said, mouthing off as if I were Van.

"I thought you said you liked the Stones?" she replied accusingly, as if she had just discovered our whole relationship had been one big lie, all twenty-four hours of it.

I, of course, hated the Stones at the time. The early Rolling Stones sounded so raw and badly recorded to me, their playing so ragged and out of tune, their beats and rhythms so simple and monotonous, I could barely make it through a single song of theirs. Unfortunately, I made the mistake of telling Ann what I really thought about her favorite band.

"They have no soul," I said, trying to sum up my educated and highly held opinion.

"How can you say that?" she yelled, louder than expected. "They're full of soul."

"I mean they sound white."

"No they don't. They're totally black."

"Have you ever heard black music?" I asked, as if that closed the case.

"You're such a snob, you know that. How can you listen to that jazz music? It sounds like everybody's playing a different song at the same time."

I was starting to get miffed. Worse, I was seeing my one and only opportunity for sex slip away like a raft in a fast flowing stream. I had to act fast or I'd be back gazing at magazines if I wanted female companionship. I switched off the record and tuned the radio to WBZN where I knew they'd be playing some acid rock, although I kept it low due to the late hour. That seemed to calm her down. At least she stopped arguing with me and started to relax. Something was different this night, something had changed, it was as if the evening before had never occurred. The jury was still deliberating my worth, the sexual ability duly noted, the answers meticulously recorded in some tiny compartment of her steel-trap mind. Now she was going to probe the depths of my psyche and soul. She didn't want to have sex. Tonight she wanted to trip.

Pulling out a small sheet of paper with little black dots on it, she tore one off and gave it to me. I immediately placed it under my tongue. This wasn't my first LSD trip, but I wasn't a big fan of Timothy Leary's brand of high. ACID felt too much like a full-blown psychosis for my taste, although back in those days we pretty much tried everything at least once. After all, it was the *Age of Experience*, the hippy era, the free sex and fast drugs generation, and Boston in the summer of 1968 was right smack in the center of it.

I used to take my tabla – Indian hand drums – down to the Commons and sit in the park. The place would be mobbed with flower children, a good percentage of them women. There's nothing like a pair of Indian hand drums – or a little dog – to attract female attention. I'd put on my brightest flowered *Beatles* shirt and most outrageous bell bottoms, hang some hippie-beads over my neck and off I'd go. I'd invariably come home empty handed, of course. Oh, I'd get close but no cigar. I'd smoke a joint or two, but nothing more than that, most of the time just pretending to be tripping. I was there to meet chicks, not scare them away.

If my powers of conversation were bad normally, they were downright dismal under the influence of most drugs. On ACID they were completely nonexistent. I might as well have been a blabbering, paranoid idiot. It was going to be a long night. Where the previous evening had been an incredible romantic fantasy, this one was a six hour marathon of psychoanalysis and interrogation. The only things missing were the glaring lights and pliers. The more she probed the more inadequate and guilty I felt.

Was this some form of masochistic torture, get a poor guy wrecked on LSD and then ask him a bunch of mind-twisting questions? At first I thought we were going to have sex. I had heard it was like having an out of body experience and was looking forward to the possibility, but that was the furthest thing from her mind. It was just as well, I couldn't have kept myself hard if I was gorged on Viagra, I was so spaced out. Everything was bugging out and getting weird, my mind and senses playing optical tricks on me that left my head spinning and me holding onto my chair for dear life, as if it was careening away in space.

I looked at my hands. They seemed to be a thousand miles away. I looked out my window into a dark, drizzling night. It seemed to sparkle with electricity and mystical, glimmering lights. The room became claustrophobic, so we wandered down wide Commonwealth Avenue toward Boston Commons where she grilled me with tough questions about my deepest beliefs. I had all I could do to recount my childhood. We wandered around in the park for awhile, until I became paranoid, and rightly so. Ending up back at my apartment just as it was getting light, I counted the minutes until I'd come down again, and kept saying to myself, "You're not going crazy. You're not going crazy." I promised if I made it through the night with my sanity intact I'd never do anything like this again. Of course I lied.

We slept through most of the next day, she on my bed after changing the sheets, me on the couch with no sheets. Later that day we went to a movie at the Charles Street Theater. She had now spent enough time with me to know me for the idiot I really was, a kid fresh from the boonies with a head full of half-notions and a bit of undirected talent. I might be a late bloomer, but she didn't have time to wait around and see. That afternoon, after sitting through the most depressing movie I had ever watched, called *Elvira Madigan*[3], she told me I had the wrong vibe. We were walking home up Newbury Street, the boutique-lined boulevard on the corner of which the theater was located.

"That was the most beautiful movie I've ever seen," she commented, tears in her eyes. "Didn't you just love the story and the scenery?"

"Yeah, especially the part where she throws-up after eating grass, that was beautiful." I was finally starting to come down from our twelve-hour trip.

"How can you joke about something like that? It was so sad, and it's a true story."

"That just makes it more depressing," I said, my nerves frayed and on edge, my judgment blurred from lack of sleep and too many drugs. I didn't mind lying and playing the sensitive guy if I was getting a little, but after the shutout of the night before I'd be darned if I'd say I liked this piece of tear-jerky sentimentality.

"I don't need to spend ten bucks to be depressed," I continued. "I can do that fine on my own, thank you. If I want to see a slice of

---

[3] The movie is about this beautiful female tightrope walker and her lover, who starve to death rather than give in to some evil government or other, and was a cult hit at the time.

tragedy and grimy life all I have to do is look out my window. When I go to the movies I want to see something funny or exciting, not three hours of that bull-crap. There should be a law against making a movie like that, or at least a warning or something."

"I had you all wrong," she said, tears welling in her eyes. The way she looked at me instantly broke my heart. I felt rejected and guilty all at the same time. I knew what was coming. I knew I had gone too far with my outburst. Then she uttered those fateful words.

"You just don't have the right vibe, Joey. You just don't have the right vibe."

I was crushed, although I had seen it coming. Ann was not only the first girl I had slept with in a long time, she was one of the most sophisticated and beautiful. It would be some time before I scored anything of that caliber again – and when that happened I married the lady.

"I'll vibrate anyway you want!" I yelled after her as she swung around the corner and out of my life just as quickly and abruptly as she had entered it. I never saw her again.

So much for predatory females.

Chapter 13

The Visit

A few days later, after recovering somewhat from my weekend of rejection, I was finally getting around to doing the dishes. It was just after eleven in the morning. I had slept late since there was no rehearsal. My roommate, Jack Adams, was still at his girlfriend's where he would end up staying all summer. I was planning my otherwise free day when there was a knock on the door.

I wasn't expecting company. Martha and Stephanie, the two bombshells who lived upstairs would come down to borrow sugar now and then, but they were out of town. The Keatings, the fun couple who lived downstairs in the basement apartment, were both at work. Anyone else would have had to ring the buzzer to get in. I opened the door and was pleasantly surprised. It was Linda, my ex-girlfriend from Plattsburgh.

"Hi, Joey. You said you could get us in to see Van Morrison if we came down. Well, here we are."

I couldn't believe my eyes. Maybe Linda had had second thoughts about me after all, and had reconsidered my invitation. Then I remembered the tall, good-looking guy she had been with last time I saw her. I certainly wasn't going to play host to those two lovebirds.

"Who are you with?" I asked suspiciously, looking around to see who was with her.

"I'm here with my friend Diane. We're here for a couple of days. Are you going to let us in or what?"

I relaxed. No boyfriend in tow.

There she was standing before me in all her beauty, in a pair of jeans with her shirt tied up to show her tanned midriff. I wanted to jump her right there. Her friend Diane was a cute little brunette with a button nose and a pert figure, who would have been the sole object of my attention had Linda not been there. As it was, I hardly noticed her, though she wore a sexy little summer outfit.

I couldn't believe my luck, two gorgeous girls at one time. Maybe playing with Van had its benefits after all.

They cooked my supper and spent the night. Linda was demure and hard to read, giving me mixed signals, which I couldn't quite interpret, but took to mean I still had a chance. Maybe she was leading me on, but I still had hope. Other than a goodnight peck on the cheek, however, as they both filed into my narrow bedroom, I was left in the cold. I entertained myself imagining what they were doing to each other - I could dream couldn't I?

The next day I told them we were playing on the North Shore that weekend, but would be rehearsing the following day if they wanted to meet Van. They said they'd love to, as they wouldn't be able to stay for the weekend. I was making all sorts of plans where to take Linda. First I'd show her around the Common where I was sort of a celebrity; then I'd take her downtown along Tremont and Washington Streets to look at the stores; then back up to Berklee, which was open for the summer session. I was planning to ask Tom to drive us to rehearsal the next day. I hardly thought to include Linda's friend, Diane, who stayed quiet and in the background. Linda remained friendly, but evasive. Then she suddenly stood up.

"I've got to go meet someone," she announced, grabbing her handbag and sweater and dashing toward the door. "You two can keep each other company until I get back. Have fun," she yelled as the door closed behind her.

I looked at Diane rather stunned.

"She didn't tell me she was meeting someone. Where's she going?" I asked rather perturbed.

"Her boyfriend, Ted, is going to school at BU. She's going to meet him. Don't worry, they'll be there tomorrow to see Van."

I didn't know what to say, and sat silently for some time as Diane, who hadn't said two words since she got there, began to sprout poetically about Linda and her boyfriend.

Well, I thought, wasn't it nice for Linda to bring a friend along to keep me company while she's gallivanting around town with some guy. Good luck seeing Van, I vowed. I was hardly listening to Diane, who was parroting everything I had said about my plans.

"Let's start with Boston Common," she suggested. "I've always wanted to see that place."

As cute and pert as Diane was, with her white blouse and dark skirt she was about as far as you could get from a flower-child. She looked like she had just stepped out of a Good Housekeeping magazine, her hair in a small beehive, with red-lipstick and nylons.

She didn't stop talking the whole time, mostly about her sisters and cousins and their many affairs of the heart. One sister was married,

71

one was engaged, and one had two boyfriends. She was between men. How convenient.

She found everything exciting and novel, gushing at every new experience. Unfortunately, the Hell's Angels were out on the Common this day, pouring beer over some hippy's head. Diane felt sorry for the guy and went over to console him. Before I knew it three hippie dudes had joined us, all invited by Diane, who would talk to any and every guy who came within earshot. She may not have been hip, but she sure knew how to attract men.

Somehow I ditched the guys and had her all to myself again by the time we got back to my apartment. She may not be Linda, but she was a bird in the hand. Later that night Linda called and said she wouldn't be back until the morning. Diane took the call, otherwise I would have told her not to bother.

Over dinner, which I cooked – steak and asparagus, my favorite dish – I regaled her with stories about Van, setting her up for the kill. It seemed to be working. We drank wine. She sat spellbound looking at me with her big blue eyes. She really was a pretty girl, and I was getting ready for a night of bliss. I thought I had struck the mother-lode when she came out of the bathroom in nothing but a short nightie.

She was exquisite, a little doll, one of those people who looks better the less they wear. She had an absolutely perfect ten body with ivory skin. I wanted her.

I tried to play it cool, as if I was used to seeing beautiful, almost naked women. I had forgotten all about Linda, and was even prepared to forgive her for this wonderful gift she had bestowed on me. I got right down to business and told her how gorgeous she was. Taking a cue from my roommate, who although not great looking got more chicks than you could shake a stick at, I asked her if she wanted to have sex, except not quite that politely.

"I thought you were Linda's boyfriend?" she said coyly.

"Linda's out with another guy!" I answered a little too vehemently. "Linda and I are old news."

"It didn't seem old last night when you were trying to go to bed with her."

"Who me? No way. What gave you that idea?"

"The way you were looking at her. You're still in love with her."

"The hell I am," I protested, knowing full well I should have given Diane more attention. Now she felt like the second choice that she was. That was before I saw you in your nightie, I almost told her. Instead, I protested my innocence.

"It's you I want," I said honestly.

"Hmm, it didn't seem like that last night. You acted like you were still in love with Linda. She asked me what she should do."

"Oh, so you're talking about me? I'm not in love with Linda. We broke up over a year ago. I'm over her. If you give me a chance I'll show you how much."

"No, I couldn't do that to a friend."

"What, you're not doing anything to Linda. She could care less. She wanted us to get to know each other."

"She told me not to go to bed with you," Diane informed me.

"What?" I cried. "That's ridiculous. Why did she say that?"

"She's afraid you'll get hurt."

"You're hurting me now, Diane. You're killing me."

"No I'm not. Go to bed. I'll see you in the morning."

With that, she gave me a full kiss on the mouth, as if you say, see what you're missing, then slipped into my bedroom and shut the door. Just to be sure, I tried it a few minutes later and called her name. It was locked.

"Go to sleep, Joey," she said from the other side.

Yeah, rats-a-ruck.

I lay awake all night totally miserable, the noises of the street keeping me from sleep, but it was too hot to close the large living room window. Diane emerged bright-eyed and beautiful around eight the next morning, and paraded around in her shear negligee until I grabbed her around the waist and kissed her. She suffered my advance good-naturedly, patted me on the arm, and went back to the bedroom to change. She had obviously gotten all the attention she craved.

After breakfast I directed her to the Laundromat around the corner so she could do some wash. Rehearsal was at one. Tom would be picking us up at twelve-thirty. It was almost noon before a buzz announced Diane was back. Shortly after that she knocked and I opened the door. To my annoyance she wasn't alone.

"Joey, this is Danny. He wants to go see Van with us."

Danny was another hippy wannabe, a bit younger and taller than me with long blond hair and girlish good looks.

"Hi, man," he said.

Of course I objected that I couldn't be bringing a bunch of strangers to John's house to see Van. I wasn't taking Linda's friend

73

and I certainly wasn't going to take hers. She got offended and said if Danny couldn't go than she wasn't going. I said that was fine with me. The next thing I knew she had taken her things and left the apartment.

She called Linda on my phone before she left and told her what a jerk I was.

"I don't know what happened to him," I could hear Linda reply on the other end of the line. "He used to be such a sweet guy."

Chump is more like it. I slammed the door behind them and gave the empty apartment a piece of my mind. I felt like used newspaper, only good to wipe your feet on. I could only hope things would get better. In the meantime, I had a big gig to get ready for.

Chapter 14

The Association

One of the biggest shows we played that summer was at the North Shore Music Theater in Beverly, Mass. The place probably held three thousand people at the time and it was packed, although they weren't exactly there to see us, at least not the majority of them. Most of the audience was there that evening to see the headliners, the group we were opening for, the band, The Association.

The Association was primarily a singing group, six guys who sang harmony and were mega big at the time with a huge hit called *Cherish*, as well as movies to their credit. Even though I knew about them and had seen them on TV - I only recognized the Hawaiian guy - the homogenized, soft rock sound left me limp.

When we played there the Music Theater had a stage in the round where the bandstand was in the middle of the theater, which ringed it like a coliseum. Each seat was slightly higher than the one in front of it in a complete circle around the stage, quite a unique and intimidating venue.

Before the show we were all together in the dressing room with the other band. They seemed like nice enough fellows. They were friendly and talkative, and they all had dark tans and gleaming smiles. I was quite impressed. They obviously knew about and respected Van, who seemed to be the center of attention. Much like when the DJs came backstage to talk to him, Van was holding court. When it was time for us to go on, I stopped by where Van had disappeared in a corner to perform his pre-concert ritual.

"They're really nice guys," I said.

"Yeah," agreed Tom, who was just behind me with his electric bass in his hands. "They're great!"

"Faggots!" replied Van.

It was time to go on. We lined up and marched down the aisle to the bandstand, through the ring of seats under the watchful eye of 3000 spectators. I was stunned. I felt like a gladiator going into combat in the coliseum. Though we would play for larger crowds that summer this was by far the most sophisticated audience, and the most intimate surroundings. I felt the pressure mount the closer we got to the stage.

As we filed down I stared sullenly at the floor and tried to block out everything but the job at hand. Tom, who had on his dark glasses as usual, looked up at the crowd like a hick in New York City, while John took it all in stride as if he belonged there.

I sat down at my drums, which were setup on a platform behind the others, and looked around at the crowd. My heart was pounding like my bass drum would be in a few minutes. I wiped my sweating palms on my pants. I had never been this nervous in my life. The lights dimmed and the announcer said his name, "And here's Van Morrison." The crowd erupted into applause, as Van strode down the aisle and jumped on the bandstand. We started out with *Domino*.

As soon as we started playing, I was aware of the incredible acoustics and sound system. This place had been built for musical performances with the performer in mind. It was like playing in a recording studio. Everything sounded alive, every instrument, his voice, perfectly balanced and fed back to us. You couldn't ask for a better sounding place to play. And play we did, hard and uninhibited, moving from old to new, one Van tune after the other, to end the show with his standards, *Gloria* and *Brown Eyed Girl*. Musically it was probably one of our best performances. The band was tight. John played exceedingly well, and Tom and I sizzled. I've seldom seen anyone on stage with such self assurance as Van that night. The reviews were great, likening Van's sound to an exciting and unique blend of blues, rock, and jazz.

The crowd's reaction was OK, not particularly wild but polite enough. I'm not sure they knew what to make of us. Our music couldn't have been more different than the band we were opening for. The Association was all vocals, with smooth, highly produced instrumentals and wide harmonies, soft and pleasant – you could hardly tell there was a drummer - while we had a hard edge and rhythmic style that was fresh and spontaneous. We played around Van's tunes as if it were a jam session rather than a concert. Heck, we didn't care. We just wanted to make music. Van sang more jazz-like that night than I'd ever heard him, using his voice like a tenor horn, scatting and improvising phrases as we drew out the endings, totally oblivious to the crowd, just getting into the mystic. It was sublime. Too bad no one taped it.

We left the stage the way we came, in a line with Van in the lead, me with my head down and a sullen look on my face, while the crowd continued to clap politely. I'm not sure if Van even acknowledged the applause. It was then I realized that even though he was a rock singer and songwriter, Van had the soul of a jazzman and that made him more than all right in my book.

My opinions would be vindicated in the coming years when he came out with all his great hits, many to become future classics. This was all in him, like a seed about to sprout, as he stood there with us laying it all out for the Music Theater crowd.

Chapter 15

The Kewpie Doll

One weekend, toward the end of the summer, we played for one of our largest crowds. It was at the Rocky Point Amusement Park in Rhode Island. The place was mobbed, thousands of people, more than I ever expected to see from a bandstand, all there to see Van.

As I looked out at the endless sea of faces, I was struck by how small I felt on that tiny bandstand, just the four of us and our instruments. It was intimidating for a minute, until I reminded myself, it's just a gig.

It was outside, a balmy summer night. Unfortunately, the sound system was terrible and we couldn't hear a thing on stage. We could not have gotten further away from the acoustics of the Music Theater if we had played in the Grand Canyon. We were using the same amps and PA system we used in John's basement, turned up to the max, to fill this huge park. As usual, the drums were un-mic'd. We had nothing like the sophisticated sound systems they have today. It was raw and unmixed

To make matters worse, I busted the head on my snare drum halfway through the first set and had to finish without it, using my tom-toms instead and making everything sound kind of African. I spent the whole next break putting on a new head and tuning it up.

We must have sounded pretty bad, everyone except Van that is. The crowd seemed to like it and screamed after every song, especially for my two favorites, *Gloria* and *Brown Eyed Girl*, both of which we played excruciatingly long versions of, while Van screamed into the microphone, his eyes closed tight, his body bent, singing his heart out in the cool evening air. It was an electrical night just for the sheer size of it and Van caught something of that electricity in his performance. It wasn't very musical, but for raw energy you couldn't beat it. Van was in his element.

He had mentioned before the gig that he was playing for a percentage of the gate and hoped the crowd would be large. He was more than pleased at the turnout. All of us expected a big payday. After all, there were four or five thousand people there, most of them screaming teenaged girls. It was loud and raucous but they loved us. It was something out of a rock and roll legend with the carnival lights in the background and thousands of spectators following our every move. The fantasy ended at the end of the night when it came time to get paid. Van handed out the usually hundred and fifty bucks.

"Is that it?" we asked. "There were thousands of people here tonight. The gate must have been fantastic, more than we've ever made before. We should get more than this."

Somehow we had gotten the impression that we were a band, you know, like the Doors or Them, even though we didn't have a name other than, 'Van Morrison and his band'. All the togetherness had blinded us to the fact that we were just sidemen, nothing but a pick-up band. We all stood there facing Van accusingly, holding our measly pay in our fists.

"They all came to see me," he said. That was the end of the discussion. None of us together could have filled my tiny bedroom on our names, let alone fill a park to overflowing. It was a lesson I never forgot, and from that moment on I understood my place. After all, it was just a gig.

Most of great performers and creative people I've met are extremely nice, grateful to be recognized and respected for their craft, and more than happy to shoot the breeze if you're polite about it. Although hard to approach, Van was no different, and would often stand around in the crowd and talk to people, and every now and then whisper into some young girl's ear.

I came close to getting lucky again that night. During a break, John, Tom, and I walked around the periphery of the park, looking at the lights and crowds, basking in our night of fame. We were followed by a bevy of pretty females, most of them flower-children and college-aged girls. One of them, a thin pretty thing with long black hair, wearing jeans with her shirt tied up like Linda's, caught my attention. She smiled at me pleasantly and exposed a little more midriff. I immediately corralled her from the pack and got her alone by the side of the bandstand.

She was a nineteen-year-old student from Emerson.

"Want to go back to my place?" I asked. No beating around the bush when you're almost a rock star.

She hemmed and hawed, and didn't want to leave her friends, but when the job ended and we were packing up the equipment, she was standing there by the bandstand smiling at me. She got a big thrill riding back to Boston in the back of the van.

Van didn't say much that night. I think he was still miffed about the band's attempted rebellion. The others were envious as usual that anyone had scored when they went home alone. The girl, whose name turned out to be Suzie, was obviously excited and didn't stop talking the whole trip home, asking questions and telling us about other bands she knew. When they dropped me off at my apartment, Suzie, who still hadn't stopped talking, went with me.

At the concert, in the colored lights of the carnival and the dark shadows of the pavilions, Suzie didn't look too bad, kind of like Steve's girlfriend Beverly on a bad hair day. In the glare of the bulb in the back of the van, however, her bad complexion and oily skin left a lot to be desired. I couldn't have cared less, and hardly took my eyes off her.

I burned some incense and lit a joint, which seemed to make her nervous, so I put it out after a few tokes. It was all downhill from there. She became quiet and sat looking around the apartment nervously. I couldn't think of a thing to say, and offered her the remainder of Ann's wine, which had sat untouched since that fateful night.

I'll never know what prompts someone like Suzie to leave her friends and get in the back of a van with a complete stranger, or what she was expecting. I suppose she considered me safe. I mean, if anything happened to her, finding Van Morrison's drummer wouldn't be difficult. Only 5000 people had seen me there. Maybe it was the need for excitement, a thrill, something to tell the gang about and make her standout from the crowd. I've never studied the psychology of a groupie, but it would make an interesting topic.

Unfortunately, I only had one thing in mind, and it wasn't conversation. I was hoping to get some action, but the only thing I'd be getting was a deep funk. If only I had known then what I know now things might have turned out better. You can be the ugliest little man on the block, but if you can talk to a woman you will never be alone.

It's an art, learned from many hard years of trial and error. Knowing what to say to draw a person out is more important than being a smooth talker. You have to show them that you are interested in what they have to say, and know enough about life and art and things to respond with intelligent and interesting comments. Making a woman feel that she is the most important person in the room doesn't hurt either. I knew none of this.

We both sat in the silence, my eyes getting heavier and heavier as she drank the remainder of the leftover wine. I eventually got the nerve to kiss her. She didn't resist, but her response was stiff and tepid. Who knows, it was probably her first time with a rock star. I checked my breath, which seemed OK, and continued the pursuit.

"Want to make out?" I asked, kissing her again. She didn't respond, but she didn't push me away either. I touched the skin of her bare midriff. She elbowed my wrist so hard I thought she broke it. We immediately parted lips and sat up stiffly. Where did I go wrong, I wondered.

She looked like she was about to be sick.

"Are you OK?" I asked in concern.

"I don't feel so good," she replied.

I got up to fetch a glass of water. As I returned with the drink she threw-up on my rug, then curled up on the couch and went to sleep. I could hardly keep my eyes open as well, and had all I could do to throw a blanket over her and drag myself to bed. I'd let my roommate's cat clean up the mess.

She left early the next morning without saying much.

Needless to say this last affair coupled with my previous rejections did not do much for my self-esteem. Here I was playing with a famous rock band and I still couldn't get any action. Let this be a lesson, learn to treat women with respect, as people not objects, and you will get a lot further than I did that late summer night. Who know, you may even make a friend.

Chapter 16

On My Own in Beantown

I guess I should explain what it was like for a kid from Plattsburgh, New York, to be dropped off in Boston - the biggest city I had ever been in outside of Montreal - and on my own for the first time in my life.

"Take care of yourself and keep your nose clean," my father told me as he was about to head back home after driving me down the previous night.

I remember the moment well. The car was parked in front of the main Berklee building on Boylston Street just before the Fens. I didn't know quite what he meant, but assumed it was something like, stay out of trouble.

That first year I lived in the dorm, in the same building that housed all the classrooms and facilities. Everything was there in that one big edifice, which had once been a hotel. Practice rooms, classrooms, band rooms, and dorm rooms, as well as offices, a cafeteria, and the library, all one big happy family.

My room was on the third floor. What a zoo. Some of the guys would become world famous musicians like Richie Cole and Harvey Mason. Some, like me, would go down in virtual obscurity. It was a heady mix to contend with my first time away from home.

My roommate was a piano player, an Italian kid. I don't remember his name, but I believe he was from Rhode Island. We hit it right off – kind of.

Before long we were gigging together with a couple of other freshman, who I would also end up rooming with in the following years. Jack Adams was a guitar player from Queens, New York, and Glenn Adams (no relation to Jack), a bass player, also, I believe, from New York. My piano playing roommate booked most of the jobs.

Here I was fresh from the boonies, but because I was from Berklee I was working steadier than I had at home where I was a sought after musician. We'd drive all over New England in the piano player's car on weekend gigs, sometimes back-to-back - dances in Rhode Island, proms in New Hampshire, the Holiday Inn in Concord, MA. It was great. Not only was I playing a lot, but I was making money. Better yet, that first year in school my parents were footing the bill. The shoe would eventually drop, but until then, although I didn't know it, this was probably the best time of my life, independent and carefree.

Although we got along well enough, living in a small dorm room with another person can be difficult, not that the piano player and I ever had as much as a cross word. Unbeknownst to me, however, I must have made him nervous.

Being a light sleeper and jealous of my night's rest, especially at 2:00 AM when I had an 8:00 AM class the next morning, I would often rage up and down the hall telling people to turn down their stereos. I just couldn't understand how some folks could be so inconsiderate as to play music – I should say *blare* music - at high decibels in a dorm room in the early morning hours. It was just plain irresponsible. Even more mystifying to me was how no one, even guys who had to get up at the same early morning hour as I did, never complained. My piano playing roommate certainly never did, and slept like a baby through the loudest of sounds.

No one was above my law when I took it into my own hands. I'd lay there despairing of sleep as someone's stereo nearby would be blasting so loud the keys on the door hook would vibrate, the bass still pounding in my head in the silence between songs. I couldn't understand why someone didn't say something. Was I the only one being kept awake? The floor warden, a senior student, was only two doors down, but he was either never there, or like my roommate, slept through the whole thing. In any case, I never wanted to knock on his door, only the perpetrators'. Even Richey Cole, the monster alto player who I later became good friends with, jamming in his Back Bay apartment, would find me banging on his door at three AM telling him to turn down the frigging stereo. He'd laugh good-naturedly, give me a quizzical look, and turn thing down. Harvey Mason, another drummer, would apologize with an engaging smile and obliged me as well, as did most of the guys, probably not even realizing they were bothering someone. Let's face it, most of us hadn't been a day out of the nest at that point.

Even though I was small I could look pretty menacing when riled, especially after losing half of my allotted eight hours of sleep. Most musicians are pacifists, but watch out for those drummers.

It would figure that the worst offenders in the dorm were the two guys in the room right next to mine. The first few times I knocked on their door and asked if they could turn down the sound almost ended in a brawl. They were two southerners, a bass player and a guitarist, 'rockers' from what I could tell, probably the worst musicians in the school, and both big guys. They were invariably bleary eyed and drunk when they answered the door, and were as rude as I was trying to be polite.

I'll never forget the first time I asked them to turn down the stereo. It was 2:47 AM. I remember because I had lain there for exactly two hours and that many minutes since going to bed at midnight waiting for them to shut it off, or for someone to tell them to. Finally, I could stand it no longer. I pulled myself out of bed, put on my pants, and went next door to plead for some peace and quiet. I had an early and important arranging class the next morning. They stood there laughing at me and tried to close the door in my face. I was doubly enraged that they did this after I had asked so nicely. That something in me that holds back the demons snapped – something from my early childhood. I forearmed the door and pushed myself into the room like a miniature tornado, shoving the laughing-boy backward. Striding in toward the stereo, I yelled.

"Turn this thing off or I'll throw it out the window."

I stood glaring at them menacingly.

Either one of them could have probably heaved me out the same window without half trying. Instead, they stood there staring at me transfixed as if I had popped out of the ground in a flaming cloud. It was no longer a matter of turning it down. The stereo was now going off or nothing.

It wasn't that I was a tough guy, although I could hold my own, but I was usually outweighed by most opponents. Being the smallest and youngest in my class all through grade school, I was the target of more than one bully. I would come running home from school every other day – we lived within walking distance – crying because one of the bigger kids had picked on me. Finally, my parents got sick of this and sent little cry baby down to Whitehall, New York to see Baba Mike, my father's dad, Mike Bebo. He was my favorite grandparent, funny and fun, and probably the scariest looking guy you'd ever want to meet, with large hands and big shoulders, and arms that seemed to reach all the way down to the ground. He was as strong as a great ape from working in the mines and on the canals and railroad, where he'd lift rock and hauled iron all day. I guess he had a bad reputation in his younger days, but he was as sweet as could be with us kids. I'm not sure what Baba Mike did or said to me, but after that one visit no one ever bullied me again. The next time someone tried, they had to pull me off the kid. The teacher came running out to the playground at all the screaming and yelling – this must have been in kindergarten – and found me on top of the bully pummeling him and swearing, "son-a-bitch, son-a-bitch." It must have been much like that classic scene in *the Christmas Story*. My parents were not amused and quite embarrassed, but not too many kids tried to pick on me after that.

They shut off the stereo and apologized, glad to see the rabid little, mad-dog drummer leave. They tried it a few more times after that, all with the same result. They blustered and threatened, but every time I called their bluff and they ended up turning it off. They finally got the picture when they complained to the floor monitor, who told them, "good for him". Maybe he wasn't sleeping all those times. It was like that all year, and while no one else complained and some like the floor warden were probably secretly grateful, it was a bit much for my poor roommate, that and the laughing.

Unlike later when I was living with Jack, I was as straight as a drum stick at this time. I mean taking aspirin and coke – the soft drink - made you a drug addict in my book. I didn't drink either. I was what you'd call on a natural high. While everyone in the dorm was either drunk out of their gourd or high on drugs, my roommate and I were momma's boys, teetotalers, although I guess I gave the opposite impression, maybe because I was always trying to be cool.

"What are you on, Bebo?" was the usual question I was asked that first year – this from the most stoned-out alcoholics in the dormitory. I would daze off and daydream while we sat at our desks doing homework in our room. I'd think of something funny, either something that happened or just a funny situation and start laughing. Nothing hysterical or anything, but like you would on hearing a good joke. I've always had a good imagination, and often used it to entertain myself with little stories and inside jokes, which I spun in my head for my own amusement. If that's crazy, I guess I was. My poor roommate obviously thought so.

This along with my nighttime antics was too much for my piano playing friend, and he opted to change rooms the first chance he got. We were still friends and worked together, but no longer shared a room and that suited me fine. I was more than happy to have the place to myself and be able to stretch out. Little did I know that I would soon wish I was back with the pianist.

85

My new roommate was a handicapped trumpeter, who came to Berklee in the middle of the term after transferring from MIT - of all places. There are probably not too many who after being accepted to the premier school of Science and Engineering in the country opted for Berklee College of Music, which only that year had become a fully accredited college.

I had seen him before I ever knew I'd be rooming with him. Herb Pomeroy, one of the top teachers at Berklee and a fine trumpet player, directed the MIT swing band at the time. One day a few of us, learning this, decided to go hear Herb's band. We had heard they had this excellent trumpet player that you just had to hear. So we walked across the bridge over the Charles to the MIT auditorium where they were rehearsing. The concert hall was mostly empty. Herb was up on stage giving the band some last minute instructions. It was a full fifteen piece group with sax, trumpet, and trombone sections, plus rhythm – piano, bass, and drums. Herb heard us come in and turned around to see who it was. On seeing us he smiled and gave a quick salute. A few of the guys, like Richie Cole, were in his workshop. Berklee cats were in the house!

They started out their first tune, an up tempo thing that would have sounded great if it had been a half-decent band, but the rhythm section was stiff and dragging, and the ensemble ragged and weak. It was pretty much what you'd expect from a group of geeks where music was a third language. Even the lowest workshop at school with the student proctors was better than this. Then this little guy on crutches stood up, adjusted his thick-rimmed glasses, put the horn to his lips, and blew.

Man did he blow. He knocked our socks off. That sloppy group of engineers came to life when he soloed. He blew our minds. The clear high notes bounced off the walls of that auditorium like plastic bullets, piercing the scales with sharp precision. We called encouragement and applauded loudly after the song. Herb turned and smiled out at us. He knew he had something here. A few weeks later the guy was my roommate.

We got along well enough. At least he didn't play his stereo after midnight, and as I said, he was a great musician. The problem was, because of his handicap, which made it difficult for him to make it down to the cafeteria, he was allowed to cook in the room. Sometimes I'd come in to the most gawd-awful smelling concoctions you could imagine, although he was always offered me some. I'd probably remember his name if we had spent more time together, but he played in the top workshop with Herb and soon left Berklee to work with some famous big band, like a lot of my classmates did, but most of these names are lost to me.

One name I'll never forget is Jack Adams. Jack, as I mentioned, was a great guitarist and my roommate that second year when I played with Van. While he was away most of that summer at his girlfriend's place, he was a good friend and a big influence on the small town boy I still was by that second year at school.

Living on our own, in our own apartment was leagues better than living in the dorm. We had found a nice one bedroom place right off the corner of Gloucester and Newbury Streets, two blocks from the Prudential building and the Jazz Workshop. Our first day there Jack tried to get me high. I don't know why he waited until then or why I said OK. Perhaps he had discovered it back home in Queens that summer. I'd been offered weed plenty of times before then, but since I was always pretending to be high anyway I never wanted to ruin my cover. This time, however, for some reason I broke down, boy did I break down.

The poor guy must have rolled and smoked a dozen joints trying to get me stoned.

"Do you feel anything yet?" he kept asking as he saw his whole bag disappear before his eyes. I didn't even get a buzz.

"I don't know," I replied, feeling no different and not knowing what to expect. He finally gave up and crashed. Wondering what the hullabaloo was about, I ate about fifty-two devil-dogs and watched a Marx Brothers movie on TV. I eventually got the hang of it.

That first weekend after moving into our new apartment Jack took me in tow to meet the other tenants in the building. I've already mentioned the two girls who lived upstairs, Marsha and Stephanie, and the nice couple downstairs. I would probably have lived there all year and not have met any of them if it wasn't for Jack. Talk about out-going.

We walked upstairs first where Jack introduced us to Marsha and her gorgeous roommate, Stephanie. First thing out of his mouth was, "Want to smoke?" We were soon all bosom buddies. Same thing happened when I followed him downstairs to meet the Keatings. They ended up turning us on. I fell instantly in love with the beautiful young newlywed. She and her husband became two more of our best friends.

87

Jack was a great musician, as I've said. He could play anything from Jimmy Hendrix to Wes Montgomery and Segovia. He used to open the big window in our living room, face his amp out onto Gloucester and Newbury, turn up the volume full blast and wail. He'd play his most outrageous Hendrix licks and generate enough feedback to fill a dozen city blocks. It wasn't long before we got a visit from two of Boston's finest, knocking on our door after a noise complaint of all things. Luckily no one was smoking anything and the police liked Jimmy Hendrix. He turned down a bit after that, but not much.

I learned a lot that year playing in workshops and attending my music courses at Berklee, and was making decent money playing around the area with Jack and other cats from Berklee like Tommy Kiebania. It was a good year, other than a few of the inevitable bumps and detours along the way. Like when my Dad called and told me I was being cut off and would have to pay my own living expenses and rent if I wanted to go to school. With this last thought constantly in my head, I tried to navigate my uncertain future.

Chapter 17

Ode to Joy and Judy

Fame is a curious thing. Some people seek it all their lives, only to find when they finally obtain it, that it has becomes a curse. Take 'Lucky Lindy', Charles Lindbergh. Here was probably the most famous person in history, who was also the most private of men. He became an instant celebrity early in his life, and spent the rest of it hiding from his fame.

Van worked hard to gain the level of respect and notoriety he has obtained, yet fights just as hard to maintain his privacy. I never thought in terms of being famous, only making good music with good musicians. Being a good player meant everything to me. Everything else was secondary. For me, a little notoriety went a long way. I finally realized that quantum of fame shortly after my disastrous evening with Suzie.

I was feeling low as I strolled down Boylston Street toward the Commons, though it was a gorgeous day and the sky was clear and blue. Except for being rejected yet again I shouldn't have had a care in the world, but I was starting to wonder if perhaps I was doing something wrong where women were concerned.

I had on a loud, colorful t-shirt and bell-bottom jeans, one of the get-ups I sometimes wore on stage. Just as I was approaching Arlington Street, a couple of girls walking in the opposite direction stopped me.

"Aren't you the drummer with Van Morrison?" asked the pretty one.

"Yeah," I said, momentarily taken aback. This was my first real moment of almost fame, being recognized and stopped on the street by perfect strangers, two women yet! Now you're talking!

"We saw you at the Tea Party. You guys are real good."

"Thanks," I replied.

"I'm Joy," said one.

"I'm Judy," announced the other.

"Hi, I'm Joe," I said introducing myself. I was in a funk and didn't have much to say, but Joy and Judy kept the conversation going well enough. Suddenly we were the three Js. They both went to BU, and like me were in town for the summer between semesters. We wandered over to the park, which was nearby, and joined the throng of hippies on the corner of Beacon and Charles streets.

I never had much luck with the college girls around town, especially BU coeds. Most of the women from the local colleges wouldn't give me the time of day, especially after I told them what school I went to. Just mentioning Berklee was usually the kiss of death unless they were art students. Then when a coed did condescend to talk to me it was like an exam.

There were no women at Berklee at that time. A few eventually started showing up toward the end of my stent there, but for my first few years there wasn't a female within sight of the school, not that it would have made any difference where I was concerned.

There seemed to be a lot of angst at the time, student protests and demonstrations and things. Everyone had one agenda or another they were trying to force on you. The guys at Berklee were for the most part oblivious to that kind of thing, although people were upset when Martin Luther King was assassinated that spring, and Bobby Kennedy a few months later. But we certainly didn't take to the streets en masse to protest.

Most of the college women I talked to questioned me on whether I believed in this position or followed that line, all political stuff. Or how was I going to change the world. Change the world, I hardly changed my socks. Thus my miserable track record in Boston's dating life - until now. Joy and Judy were different, perhaps because they saw me playing with Van.

My roommate Jack was still living at his girlfriend's, so I had the three-room apartment to myself. There was no food or wine in the place and it was a mess, but the invitation was out of my mouth before I knew what I was saying.

"Want to come over to my place?" I asked, looking at Joy, whose long auburn hair hung halfway down her back. She wore a mini-dress with a high hem and a low neckline, which showed plenty of pretty leg and bosom. She smiled provocatively at me.

"Sure, that sounds like fun!" answered Judy, who had dark hair and brown eyes and was on the plump side. A little too big-boned for my taste and taller than I was, she looked like she could have squeezed me to death with her thighs.

We walked back up Commonwealth Ave to my pad and up the short flight of stairs past the first floor insurance office. On the way up we met Marsha, the bombshell on the third floor, coming down.

"Hi, Joey," she said, as she skipped down the stairs in her short-shorts. "I saw you with the Association last weekend. You guys rocked. I'd love to meet Van."

"You should have come backstage," I replied, happy to be talking about Van in front of the BU girls.

"I'd *really* like to meet one of those guys from the Association. What a bunch of hunks."

"You want to join us," I offered. "I'm going to get a bottle of wine."

I had to ask even though I hoped she'd decline. After all, you never knew who you were going to meet hanging with Stephanie and Marsha[4]. Thankfully she declined.

"Got a date," she informed us as she bounced the rest of the way down the stairs, wiggling seductively in her too-short shorts.

I opened the door to my apartment and let my guests in. While they stood and admired the high-roofed ceiling and hardwood floors, I rushed around and picked up scattered underwear and dirty t-shirts, and burned two sticks of incense – much cooler than air-freshener.

Once that was done I offered them some coffee, the only beverage I had in the house, which they accepted. I then asked them if they smoked pot, calculating my meager supply would just about be wiped out with one good-sized joint. I needn't have worried.

"Sure," said Judy, pulling out a pack of Jobs and a baggie full of dark green buds. She swiftly poured some of the stuff into a paper and sprinkled a few chunks of a dark, tar-like substance on it.

"What's that?" I asked, curious as to what I was about to be inhaling.

"Opiated hash," said Judy, lighting up her creation with a long wooden match.

I put on some mood music, a vintage Ravi Shankar record – Indian jazz - and took a toke from the cigar-shaped spliff, holding it in as long as I could. I was instantly racked by a ragged coughing jag. The

---

[4] During the filming of the *Boston Strangler* they dated and partied with the stunt crew. Marsha even obtained the ultimate trophy through her irresistible charms, Tony Curtis's briefs nailed to her bedroom wall.

room started spinning. I saw swirling stars. Exhaling hard, I grabbed the arms of my chair.

"Wow!" I stammered, trying to right my equilibrium. "That's good stuff!"

I couldn't have taken more than two tokes, but I was flying higher than a hang-glider off Mount Everest. The picture on the wall came to life, the horses moving, the trees waving. I felt like I had just dropped LSD. My perspective was skewed, the colors unreal.

Drugs were as much a social thing in the counterculture community of Boston in 1968 as alcohol was in the madmen days of the fifties, a way to relax and meet people, which is ironic considering the antisocial effect it had on me. I found it hard to meet and talk to people stoned out like a zombie, but it was a good come-on, at least on this occasion. We ate pasticcios and watched the Three Stooges on my small, black-and-white TV for the rest of the afternoon. I could hardly get a word in edgewise between the two of them as they bantered back and forth and played titillating mind games with me.

Much to my surprise they returned the next day and became regular fixtures around my apartment. Boy did I have the hots for Joy. I would have done anything to get in bed with her. Of course, Judy was the one who had the crush on me. Joy was obviously only there to help her friend. I played along, hoping I'd get lucky. Alas, it was not to be

It was a funny triangle, me after Joy and Judy after me. If I had played my cards right I might have had both of them, but then I was a lamb in wolf's clothing. I never had a chance. They were great girls and fun company, and somewhat renewed my faith in the opposite sex. There would be many more episodes with Joy and Judy, but that's another story.

Chapter 18

Death in the Catacombs

Van has evolved over the years like all good artists, at least those who have any staying power. Never content to rest on his laurels, he was always striving for something new, something different. In spite of the fact that he had two hits under his belt, which we played everywhere we went, he never tried to copy them. All his newer songs were more sophisticated both lyrically and harmonically. The jazz influence in his music was also becoming more pronounced with songs like *Moon Dance,* which we were starting to rehearse, and as would be seen in the early Warner Brother's albums and later with Bluenote. In my opinion, Van is one of the most honest performers you will ever hear.

Thinking back on it, I can say it was a rich experience. I cherish the time I got to work with the man. I can't listen to one of his songs and not think about that summer forty-six years ago and how much his music has meant to so many people. Despite the years, the memories of those times remain vivid, as if it had happened yesterday.

I've done many different things over the intervening time, but those few months have enriched my life in a way that's hard to describe. It's being a part of something bigger than yourself, of something that will outlast you. Of course, I didn't realize any of this at the time. It was just a gig to me, a way to support myself through the summer. Then we'd see what would happen. I wasn't thinking much further ahead than that.

Van kept the band working. A week didn't go by where we weren't playing in one place or another, some good, some bad, but always interesting. The more we played as a group, no matter the little glitches, the better and tighter we sounded. Sometimes, however, we didn't get to play at all.

We were working at a place called the Catacombs, a small club on upper Boylston Street, just before the Fens, right next to Berklee, which has since moved to Mass Ave just around the corner. It was great for me, because I could roll out of class and be at the gig. They usually had folk music there. I'd stop by and listen through the open door once in awhile to the music coming up the dark staircase, but nothing ever caught my fancy and I'd walk by. This weekend it was our turn to keep people from walking by, though we were about as far from a folk band as you could get.

We were strictly electric. We would have no more thought of playing acoustically than we would have thought of playing in the nude, but sometimes things don't turn out as planned.

If you've ever played with an electric band, one with amplifiers and cords, you've probably experienced the Grinch that stole the show, the one that turns up just before curtain time and gums things up. Well, that's what happened to us on our opening night at the Catacombs.

The place was dark inside as befitted its name, with black walls and dim lights, like a cave. There were small tables scattered around the floor and along the walls. The stage consisted of a raised, square platform stuck in the corner by the door. I sensed something was wrong the minute we got up on the bandstand.

Van was sitting at a table near the stage waiting to go on, looking at Tom with a mildly concerned expression. Tom was fiddling with his bass. Every time he jiggled a cord there'd be a loud bark from his amp. Not a good sign, but I didn't give it much thought as I sat down to adjust my set.

There was a good crowd, even for early on a Friday night. The soft banter of the audience mingled with the sound of tinkling glass. This was one of the more intimate venues we had played all summer. Instead of a sea of kids standing and yelling, this audience was sitting down and quietly sipping drinks, a sophisticated crowd of true music aficionados, all together in a small room. It was like we were back in John's basement again. We were all looking forward to playing. There was a feeling of anticipation in the air, like something special was about to happen, a feeling of expectation and possibility. Joy and Judy showed up to take a table near the bandstand. Tom's amp continued to pop and burp every time he touched his cord. It was starting to become annoying.

The witching hour was fast approaching. It was time to play. Every table and seat in the joint was taken and still people were coming in. I tested my drums, laying down a rhythm with my hi-hat, snare, and bass, using the rim of my snare to accent the off-beat. I was suddenly drowned out by a series of loud barks and burps from Tom's bass that brought peoples' hands to their ears. Tom rushed to shut off his speaker and Van shot up from his chair like it was hot.

All four of us were on the bandstand now. Tom pulled out a tangled jumble of cords, half knotted together, but after ten more minutes of trying he still couldn't get any of them to work. The few that did made loud, intermittent noises, which made it impossible to play. We were dead in the water, like a boat without a rudder.

We waited as Tom tried different jacks and connections, at one point taking out a soldering gun, but nothing seemed to work. The crowd was forgotten in our frantic efforts to get Tom's amp working. He labored on his hands and knees with his tools and a small flashlight like a surgeon working over a comatose victim, all to no avail.

"I'll have to see if I can get another amp," he said suddenly, getting up and running off the stage. "I'll see if anyone at school has one." Then he was gone, rushing out into the damp night air and across the street to the dorm.

Van disappeared into the dressing room, a closet-sized cubical behind the bandstand, while John talked to a couple of girls sitting at the bar. I whiled away the time with Joy and Judy. Looking around, all I saw were disappointed, impatient faces, upset at being charged a cover fee to get in and then being kept waiting. Things were going from bad to worse.

Tom returned about the time our first set should have been ending, bearing a new amp. By that time the crowd had thinned considerably. He spent the next half hour trying to get the new piece of equipment, which he was unfamiliar with, working. All he could elicit from the stubborn thing was a series of atrocious buzzing sounds and feedback. It was the first time I ever wanted to shove a drumstick in someone's ear.

Finally, after a mind boggling series of experiments with different cords, connectors, and amps, Tom was able to get his bass working. Now it was time for Van's PA to kick out on us. It seemed that every single electrical device in the place was conspiring against us.

Most of our equipment was pretty primitive, even for the times. Tom and John each had their own amplifiers and speakers, which together were about the size of a large bureau. Van's PA consisted of a small amp with two medium-sized speakers, both of which we aimed out at the audience. Even when it was cranked up to the max it could hardly fill an auditorium. I of course was completely unmic'd. Steve and Andy could carry the equipment and set it up, but neither was capable of troubleshooting the electronics. In any case, they wouldn't be back until closing. We were on our own.

By this time there were only a handful of diehard fans left in the club, hoping for at least one Van Morrison set before they had to trek out into the dark stormy night. The way it was going they might have to wait all evening.

John and Tom were finally able to get the PA working again by running it through the borrowed amp. Somewhere during his struggles Tom had obtained his upright, which he ran through the other working amp along with John's guitar. When Van finally started singing we did what amounted to an acoustic set, working on some of the newer tunes almost as if it were a rehearsal. We played soft and jazzy behind Van's wailing vocals. I even grabbed the brushes for a few pieces, and laid my stick across the rim of the snare a lot, things I never did with the band even in John's basement. Our seventeen-year-old guitarist played with a folksy style using his fingers and picking the strings instead of strumming them violently like he usually did. It was a nice quiet ending to what started out as a stormy night. John Payne, a sax player from school, joined us on flute halfway through the set. The dozen or so people in the crowd seemed to like it, and didn't leave till the last note. Even *Brown Eyed Girl* was enjoyable.

Van didn't once complain and seemed to enjoy what little music we got to play. He must have gotten paid despite the missed sets. Who knows, these events may have had some impact on his next album, Astral Weeks, which was all acoustic, not one stinking amp!

The next night at the club was a little better, with a small but appreciative crowd and a sound system that worked. Peter Wolfe, the local radio celebrity was there, eagerly awaiting Van's debut in this unusual setting. Because of the intimate size of the room and the nice acoustics, we were able to play jazzier than usual. Tom continued to use his upright. Even John played with some taste that weekend. John Payne joined us again as well on flute, and would end up on Van's next album. The reviews for that weekend were decent even if not good enough for Van. We played there a couple of times that summer. Despite the lousy start, the Catacombs became one of our favorite places to work.

Chapter 19

A Musician's Life

Perhaps I should give you an idea what it's like to be a real working musician, lest you get the wrong impression with all this rock and roll glamour. By the time I was living with Jack, we were no longer working with the guys I had gigged with the previous year.

I was playing with pickup bands doing everything from strip clubs to society gigs, as I would do after Van. Contrary to my fears earlier that summer, I would have no trouble supporting myself through the next three years of school and thereafter playing drums.

There were a couple of agents around town at that time who kept me working fairly steady. They liked me because I could play anything. I was a big favorite of the girls at the strip clubs in the combat zone. I would kick the drums in time with their gyrations and get those tom toms thumping and those cymbals crashing to their bumps and grinds. I never took my eyes off them. It was like playing a three hour drum solo.

The society gigs were always interesting. Usually in grand ballrooms, or ritzy hotels, or yacht clubs, where we'd dress to the max in rented tuxedos and play to the cream of Boston society. That was me, in the combat zone one night, at the Ritz the next.

You never knew who you'd bump into at one of these pickup gigs. One night I was setting up my drums next to the piano with the skyline of Boston below me, and who sat down at it but Jann Hammer, who was also at Berklee at the time. Jann, like Miroslav Vitous, was already famous before he got to the school. He would leave in a year and go on to world renown, writing, scoring, and playing music for the Miami Vice TV show. In the meantime, here he was playing two-step and bossa novas with me for an elite audience of PhDs and philanthropists.

Jann carried the whole band, although under the circumstances there wasn't much we could do. We had a horrible electric-bass player, some kid who probably had three lessons. He didn't know any of the songs and had lead ears. He couldn't hear a cord-change if he stepped on it, which he did all night. I would have given half my night's pay for

Tom that evening. I guess I wasn't playing that well either. My drums sounded like they were in a deep well. I never did feel comfortable, despite Jann's playing. He wanted me to take control like a lot of drummers do, who would just as soon play by themselves, while I was laying-back, listening. I guess not everyone likes a listening drummer.

Those society gigs could get pretty bad. A pickup band put together on the fly at the last minute might have the best or the worst of musicians. You just never knew. Sometimes the agent himself would come and either sit-in or conduct the band.

I remember one night, close to Christmas or New Year of 1968 – after Van - when I was playing a job at the Ritz Carlton, in their big room, with a twelve-piece orchestra. We were up on the bandstand and Martin Richards, the agent, was directing. In the audience were Boston politicians with their wives and supporters, along with industrialists and some military brass, all dressed to the hilt. In the band were guys like Richie Cole and my ex-roommate trumpet player from MIT.

Martin used to like to pretend that he was one of those big-time band leaders like Arty Shaw or Benny Goodman. He'd stand there and wave his arm back and forth, looking on benignly at the dancers. We would basically ignore him. He played soprano and would hold it under his arm as he conducted with the other, but with guys like Richie Cole in the band, he didn't dare play it. At one point he had Richie get up in front of the orchestra to do an alto solo – he did the same thing to the poor trumpet player on the spur of the moment, making him hobble down so fast on his crutches he almost fell. It was an old swing tune, maybe even a hipped-up version of a Christmas song, I don't quite remember. What I do remember is what happened next.

As inappropriate as it was, Richie did a solo, something like you'd hear in an elevator, doing a Guy Lombardo imitation. Martin, not getting the gag, liked it and wanted him to play more. As Richie turned around to go back to his seat, Martin yelled.

"More, more, keep playing."

Martin Richards was a funny dude. He had thick, black-rimmed glasses, with greased-down black hair, which he combed over to make it look like he wasn't going bald. He was short with a pointed nose, and talked with a rasping voice, often spitting when he got excited – Danny Devito is a good imitation. He smoked like a fiend – a pot fiend that is. He even put me to shame. He would run out between every set to get high. I'd go to his house in the suburbs to pick up my pay or see about a job, and he'd be chain-smoking reefers one after the other as we talked. His ashtray would be full of half-smoked joints.

Sometimes Martin would take his wife, who was a singer, to the gig. He'd let her sing a chorus, then when he wanted a solo he would swoop in and elbow her sharply away from the microphone. The first time I saw him do it I almost fell off my drum stool, and thought it kind of rude. She was a big, statuesque blonde, who could have knocked Martin off the bandstand with one swing of her hip, but she took it well.

Richie Cole wasn't Martin's wife, however, and when Richards started yelling at him over the band to play another solo, Richie looked at him as if he were a madman. I thought he was going to sock him right there or walk off the bandstand. Instead, he elbowed Martin away from the mike and started blowing his alto into it. Man did he blow - a string of notes up and down a dozen scales so fast and loud and smooth it seemed impossible. Richie Cole can play a lot of notes in a short time and he outdid himself that night. He huffed and puffed and blew the house down. We kept on playing but we were all on auto-pilot, watching him, mesmerized. It was astounding. I mean, it was like seeing a guy punch someone so fast that you couldn't see his hands. All you could hear were the popping of his notes like fists. Man did he put on a show.

By this time everyone had stopped dancing and was standing on the floor looking up at the bandstand not knowing what to think. It was certainly nothing anyone could have danced to. Finally, when Richie was finished, he marched back to his seat. Martin just stood there with his mouth open, not believing his ears. He had stopped conducting halfway through Richie's musical tirade. The band started clapping as did some in the audience, as Martin Richards announced, "Richie Cole, everybody. Richie Cole."

They'd hear more of that name.

Once in awhile someone at Berklee would form their own group and book gigs around town. Shortly after I worked with Van, I hooked up with a singing bass player named Paul LeGrande. He was a good-looking kid around my age, twenty-one or two, with blond hair and a thin matching mustache. Nice voice and very personable, he was also a good agent. He was on his way to stardom. Unfortunately, like many of my classmates – to my amazement – he was married and already had a kid with another on the way. I guess you could say he had added incentive.

I don't know where he got him, but Paul found this absolutely fantastic piano player. The guy wasn't from Berklee, but except for that time with Jann, I hadn't played with anyone that could tickle the keys better. What chops! An American, but recently returned from Germany with his stunning Bohemian wife, he was another one of those guys who just carried you along. It's hard to explain what it's like playing with a good, strong keyboard player. The piano embodies all of the musical notes and chords, but is classified as a percussion instrument, and for a listening drummer like me, there's nothing like comp'ing behind a good keyboard player. Time becomes a thing of beauty.

We bought matching suits and rehearsed in Paul's apartment. I didn't complain because the music was fun and the gig a good one. We were the house band in the Sheraton Prudential where we played nothing but jazz standards. What a nice gig, eight to twelve in a five-star room, full every night, top money. You never knew who would walk into the joint, people like Dizzy Gillespie – I got to hand him his trumpet - and Peter Falk. It was nice while it lasted, but like all good things it came to an end when Paul left school to follow his dream. I never heard of him again, which happens a lot in this business.

Then there were the show bands. I really worked for my money on those gigs. Usually a seven-piece band consisting of trumpet, trombone, and sax, with a rhythm section and a guitar or two, they always had the ubiquitous front man. You could hear them playing down in the combat zone opposite the go-go dancers. The Downtown Room and the Two O'clock Lounge were two of the clubs at which I used to play.

Show bands were hard work. Usually you had to wear a uniform, rehearse, and play Saturday matinees. The repertoire was mostly Rhythm and Blues and soul music, like Aretha Franklin and James Brown, which I loved, with some Chicago or Blood Sweat and Tears thrown in. Playing over two brass and as many saxes and guitars, all mic'd or amplified, should not be underestimated. Playing as hard as I could, I could barely make myself heard over all the noise. I was usually drenched after the first song and spent my breaks toweling off while the other guys bantered with the go-go dancers. That's why I admired Louie Peterson's playing so much. He could make it pop and sizzle without even breaking a sweat.

Unlike Van, it seemed like every show band front man I worked for thought they were God's gift to music. What a bunch of prima-donnas. They were usually ball-busting, a-holes who didn't know a downbeat from a hoof beat. They were nothing, however, compared to the club owners. I don't want to call them gangsters, but these guys would make the whole band take uppers if they didn't think you were lively enough. Let us say they'd give you an offer we couldn't refuse. I won't even go into the gigs out on Revere Beach where the bullet-proof plate glass in front of the Surf was covered with dents.

That's the thing with music. It's a fun way to make a living, and times were good in the '60s. It wouldn't always be that way. When the economy turns bad, live musical entertainment is one of the first things to feel the pinch. But I didn't worry about that. I lived in the moment like an errant Zen monk.

1968 had been an eventful year and Boston a valuable learning experience. Then Van came to town.

Chapter 20

Demo Tapes and Victor the One-Armed Drummer

During the latter part of the summer, a few weeks before the fall semester would start at Berklee, we went into a recording studio to cut some demo tapes. Van was looking for a label and wanted to get a good recording of the band, as well as showcase some of his new songs. He wanted to put out another album.

I was unaware – as usual – but Van must have resolved his legal battle with Bang Records, because he was actually making demos for Warner Brothers Studio in New York City. I didn't have a clue, but I knew something was up. We were in a studio!

He hired a place in downtown Boston, I think it was ACE, behind the theater district in the seedier part of town. We spent a good week there rehearsing and recording. This was a totally new experience for all of us, except Van. By then the band was really tight. Van performed in the studio as he did on stage, with the same intensity and self-induced pain. After the session we'd listen to the tapes. It sounded pretty good. The boss seemed to like it.

We did a couple cuts of Domino and another tune called Lorna. Van played some nice harmonica behind the rhythmic groove laid down by John, Tom, and me. Each of us was mic'd separately and behind a partition. Playing in the studio was great. My drums sounded sharp and alive, and of course they could mix things to emphasize one instrument or another.

By this time Van seemed sure of himself, as if he had no doubt of the outcome of things. He remained focused and intent on his goal. Boston was merely a way station, a place to regroup and revitalize. He always seemed to have his sights set on the light at the end of the tunnel. Maybe he realized this was an important turning point in his career. He had already had two mega-hits in the US, and was on the threshold of four decades of impressive creative output, destined to write a string of songs that would become modern standards. There's something about his music that just grabs you instantly. Of course, I had no inkling of any of this at the time.

People seem to either love Van Morrison or they hate him. There's little in between. I've seldom met anyone who's heard his music and are neutral, although the majority appear to be big fans. Maybe it's because his voice is so distinctive, maybe it's because his music is so truthful, without pretension or hype. Perhaps it's because of his jazzy blues style. Whatever it is, Van leaves little room for ambivalence.

It was at the recording sessions that I got to hear him close for the first time. This wasn't like the gigs where everything was so loud and chaotic that he was just a thread in a wild tapestry of sounds barely audible through my own playing. In the studio, listening to the tapes after the session, I got to hear how he used his unique voice to mold his thoughts and words into powerful emotions and images.

Yeah, this guy's a player I thought, listening to him scat phrases through the verses of his tunes. It was at that moment that I truly became aware of how good he really was. The guy had an amazing ear.

Apparently, although we all liked the way it sounded, the studio guys, the engineers and producers at ACE, didn't think I played heavy enough for rock. They wanted Van to try one of the drummers they knew and worked with, a one-armed dude named Victor. Unbeknownst to me, one day Van took them up on it and I got the day off.

I was more than happy to go on a lark and spend some of my hard-earned cash. Going shopping on expensive Newbury Street with Joy and Judy, I bought more clothes than I had purchased in the last four years, most of it for the stage. I got some colorful shirts and bellbottoms, and a brown velvet Nehru jacket with a pair of matching leather boots to go with it.

The next day I learned that while I was loafing like a fool, another drummer was auditioning for my spot, although I didn't think much about it at the time. To me it was no big deal. The way Van explained it made it all cool.

He was very upfront about it. The producer wanted a heavier rock sound.

"So they brought in this guy named Victor," Van informed me. "He's playing in some local group. He's only got one arm."

"What?" I said, surprised the guy could play drums with that kind of handicap. This was long before the drummer from Def Leopard came on the scene. "How can he play with one arm?" I asked.

"He's got a strong backbeat," Van replied.

As a matter of fact, as Van expressed it in his inimitable way, he was a bit miffed that anyone would try to tell him how he should sound, or who he should play with. He didn't seem that impressed with Victor despite the fact that he had overcome such a grave handicap to play. The cat was a lot more famous than I would ever be around town, recording with a popular local band. But Van wasn't looking for a rock sound as would soon be evident with the release of his next album.

It was during the end of these recording sessions that Van asked us if we wanted to go with him after the summer. Although I was not privy to his business dealings, I had the distinct impression that something had happened over the week of cutting demo tapes, and that he had gotten a contract with a record company, which turned out to be Warner Brothers.

We were sitting in a semi-circle in the middle of the studio.

"Do you guys want to go with me?" he asked.

The three of us looked around at one another to see what the other would say. I could hardly believe it. Van was really something. Here he was on the verge of a major success and he was more than willing to take us along with him.

John said he was sorry, but he had to go back to school in the fall. After all, he was only seventeen and still lived with his parents. I heard he went on to play and write songs for James Taylor. Van was more than understanding. Tom, bless him, was all excited and said yes on the spot. Van seemed fine with that as well. I was a bit surprised at the offer, and despite my earlier certainty was having doubts about going back to school.

"Gee, Van, I hadn't thought about it," I responded. "Can I think it over and let you know in the morning?"

"Sure," he replied. "No problem."

You couldn't ask for a more understanding guy.

It was going to be a long night. What had been a foregone conclusion at the beginning of the summer would turn out to be the most difficult decision of my life.

Chapter 21

The Choice

As I may have mentioned, I was the first in my family to go to college. No one on either side of my parents' immediate families had gone. It was a big deal, as my father kept telling me when he drove me down to Boston that warm fall night.

He had worked hard all his life to provide for my mother and us four kids, of whom I was the oldest, mostly in the construction business as a steam-fitter and plumber, trades he learned after the war. He also owned a liquor store and a motel at one point, working two, sometimes three jobs at once to try and get ahead and give his family the things he never had. He was a self-made man who built a successful life from nothing. Of all the things he wanted most for his children was to give them the tools they'd need to succeed in life, and to him nothing assured that better than a college education.

He always regretted that he didn't go to college on the GI Bill instead of learning a trade and starting a family. He said he probably could have done a lot better working half as hard if he had gotten a degree like some of his buddies did, who were now wardens of prisons and heads of corporations.

Of course, being the self-centered, selfish, know-it-all seventeen year old kid that I was I hardly listened to him, and I certainly didn't care. All I cared about was music and girls. If I thought ahead it was only to my next hamburger and gig. I had little responsibility and wanted even less. My attitude led to constant contention with my poor dad.

"Don't you care about your future," he asked one night as we were talking about where I would go to school. My grades had been dismal the first couple years of high school, but I had turned them around enough to consider continuing on to some form of high-level education, although any kind of prestigious, ivy-league school was out of the question.

To me it was a foregone conclusion, like most things in my life. My chosen profession since age eleven was drummer, and my medium of choice – jazz music. For me Berklee was the only option, but my parents were less than enthused.

"You can't play jazz all your life," my dad had insisted - this the one who had dragged us around the North Country to hear every jazz band that came within fifty miles.

"Why not?" I responded. "I make more money playing music in one night than most kids make all week with their odd jobs. I know lots of guys making a living playing in clubs."

"That's no living. Only one in a thousand make it big. It's a hard life. Your mom and I think you should go to computer school. They have courses in the State College here in New York."

"Computer school? You've got to be kidding. I want to do creative stuff, not program some stupid computer to add numbers all day. That's the most ridiculous thing I've ever heard."

I should mention that I have a Master's Degree in Computer Science and program computers for a living. At the time, however, back in 1966 when I was a seventeen year old senior in high school, computers were just about the squarest, most boring thing I could imagine. I was an artist. I had no idea how fun and creative it could be to work with computers. That was light-years in the future. Somehow, however, that future was all contingent on the decision I would be making in the next twelve hours, as I contemplated my life in the fall of 1968.

The conversation with my father had continued.

"Well, I'm not shelling out thousands of dollars for you to go down to Boston and play jazz and take drugs all day."

"Who said anything about drugs? Why'd you have to bring drugs into it?"

"Because the kind of music you listen to is drug addict music. That Charley Bird, what's his name, OD'd on the stuff."

"Dad, what's that got to do with anything? It's not true anyway. The cat was sick, man. Anyway, there's nothing wrong with the music I listen to. It's the most demanding type of music there is. It's too hard to play it well if you're all doped or boozed up. Anyone knows that."

Of course, I had absolutely no idea what I was talking about, but it sounded good.

"Well, if you insist on going to Berklee you'll have to go as an Education Major," he informed me. "At least that way you'll have a teaching degree to fall back on."

"I don't want to teach. I want to play. Who wants to teach stupid kids."

"Jesus, you have a terrible attitude. Why can't you let up and agree with me for once in your life. Don't you care about anything?"

"Yeah, I care about a lot of things, just not computers and teaching."

"Well, you're not going to Berklee unless you go as an Education Major, and you better work hard. You'll be the first person in our family with a college degree."

I had heard it a hundred times before and dismissed it as so much grown-up talk. I didn't need the pressure, but at the same time something about it sparked an ember of excitement, as if it was a chance to head off into the unknown on a great adventure.

I went home that evening after the studio session weighed down with doubt. Never one to look more than two days ahead, now I tried to gaze into the future and figure out what I really wanted to do with my life.

As long as I could remember I wanted to be a musical performer. I dreamed of being on stage playing my instrument and entertaining people with my music. The sound of the music was reward in itself, but the sound of an audience applauding for you, as I heard them do for great performers as a young boy, is something I dreamt about. The college education had been a later, secondary goal, more my parents' than mine. Now the two were facing off and only one would be left standing.

The last month playing with Van had been as close to those dreams as I had ever come. Granted, it wasn't exactly me they were clapping for, but I was part of it. Playing in front of thousands of people in places like the amusement park in Rhode Island and the Music Theater with the Association, and the week in the recording studio, had begun to turn my head. I was so close to fame I could taste it. Going to class, practicing with drum pads and metronomes, playing in workshops where you were lucky to end a tune without being stopped, all seemed to pale when compared to being on stage with Van.

I tried to remember the perspective I'd had earlier - it's just a gig - but it wasn't just a gig anymore, it was an experience, and part of me wanted it to never end.

I had never practiced looking ahead, planning for a future I only half believed in. Now I found it as difficult to do as I thought it would be. Like my rudiments, I should have practiced more. I could see nothing but tedious, boring work ahead of me, all toward a reward I already had in hand. Not being used to seeing beyond my nose, I couldn't see the end of that seemingly endless road. Two more years of school, three if I changed my major, seemed like a lifetime to me. Going with Van was looking better each minute. Maybe I'd be on his next album, I mused.

I thought of calling my parents, but knew they would only make the decision more difficult. I had heard how important a college degree was all my life. I appreciated what kind of opportunity it was, but I had also been exposed to the fame and glory that music can bring, and how through it one person can touch millions, exactly like Van was doing now with me behind him. *That* was a once and a lifetime opportunity as well.

The more I thought about it the more difficult the decision became. I needed guidance.

I decided to go downstairs and see my friends the Keatings. They were older and wiser and always had good advice. Besides, Diane was hot and would probably invite me to dinner if I timed it right.

They were both home and just about to sit down to the table. John invited me in and asked if I'd eaten. Diane had made spaghetti and meatballs, my favorite. They were both big Van Morrison fans and had seen him earlier that summer on the Commons before I joined the band.

"So how's it going with Van?" John asked as I twirled a long string of pasta on my fork.

"Good," I said as I chewed. "Where were you last weekend?" I wiped my mouth with a napkin and took a sip of wine. They had never seen me play. "We were at the Catacombs. I thought you were coming."

"We didn't get home till late Friday," Diane answered. "Tony and Sue came over Saturday night. Marsha and Steph came down. We knocked on your door to invite you and Jack until we remembered you were working. Sorry."

"That's all right. We'll be there next weekend. I'll get you in free."

"Great, we'll be there."

"Hey, guess what," I continued. "Van asked me if I wanted to go with him."

"No kidding," said John. "That's great. Are you going?"

"I don't know. He asked the whole band. John's going back to school, I think. Tom's going, though. I think Van's going to cut a record with Warner Brothers out in LA."

I was still under the impression they were headed to LA for some reason, maybe because Warner Brothers' movie studios was out there.

"Wow, that's quite a change of scenery," observed Diane, going to pour me another glass of vino. I held my hand over the glass and declined.

"I've got to keep a clear head. I have a big decision to make. What do you think I should do?"

"Go!" said John loudly. "Are you crazy? That's a great opportunity!"

"I know, but I'm kind of committed to finishing school."

"You can always go back to school. You may never get a chance like this again."

"I don't know," cautioned Diane. "That's why he's going to Berklee. He'll get to play with a lot of people."

"Not people like Van Morrison," John insisted. "*Gloria's* the best song ever written."

I'd been through this before with him, but tonight I had bigger things on my mind than arguing the merits of a song.

"It's not as simple as that," I countered. "If I leave school my father won't pay for it anymore."

"Go for it, man," urged John, finishing his glass of wine with a flourish. "You'll regret it if you don't."

"Just do what you think is right," said Diane with a sweet smile.

I thanked them for dinner and the advice and went back to my apartment, but it was suddenly too small to contain my dilemma. I had to get out of the claustrophobic space. Throwing on a jacket, I jogged down the stairs and out into the cool night. Who would I bump into on the street but my roommate, Jack Adams.

"Hi, Jack," I said. "How you been? Haven't seen you in awhile."

"Good, just came to pick up a few things."

"You're not moving out are you?"

"No, just trying it with Nancy for the summer. I'll be back in the fall. How's the gig going? Need a guitar player?"

"No, why, want me to break John's arm?" I joked.

"No, Bebo, that won't be necessary. If there's any arm breaking to do, I'll do it."

"Hey, Van asked us to go with him."

"What, the whole band?"

"Yeah, cool, heh?"

"Yeah. Where's he going?"

"LA, I think, to cut a record. What should I do?"

"What about school?"

"I don't know. What about it?"

"Well, don't you want to get your degree?"

"Yeah, kind of, but this Van thing could turn out big. Who knows what could happen. I could end up on his album."

"Do you have a contract?"

"Well, no, things are kind of informal."

"Seems a bit uncertain to leave school for."

"Sometimes you have to take risks to get ahead. This could be a big opportunity."

"It could be a big mistake. What did your parents say?"

"I haven't told them, but my Dad said he couldn't continue paying my tuition if I left school and tried to go back. I'd have to do it on my own."

"That's expensive, man, a couple grand a semester. You can afford that?"

"Hey, if I'm working with a rock star I might, that and a whole lot more."

"I thought you wanted to play with some good cats."

"Who knows who I'll be playing with."

"Yeah, and who knows where. Good luck. I gotta go. See you later. If you split you have to help me find a roommate."

Jack headed into the apartment and I turned right toward Commonwealth Ave, a couple blocks down Gloucester, and from there on toward the Commons.

Somehow being out in the open, walking down the broad avenue with the cars and lights and people cleared my mind. I looked up at the stars. There was the Prudential, towering over the peaks of dozens of apartment buildings. Suddenly I felt small.

I thought of my father and mother and their parents before them, and felt even smaller, a tiny link in an endless chain, all those lives before me leading to this place and time - to me.

I'm not sure why, but I started crying, perhaps from happiness, but more likely from homesickness. I felt like I lived a charmed life. I didn't know who to thank, so I thanked God. I felt fortunate, but at the same time as if I owed a debt. I somehow had to repay all those people who had gone before me and given their blood and sweat and toil and tears, but especially their love, for the next generation. I couldn't throw all that away. I had to contribute something. I knew then that I would always cherish the memory of this summer, but that I had to continue on the journey I had started and finish school.

I ran back to the apartment and called my parents, who had no idea of the revelations I'd just had or how close I came to quitting college. They were happy to hear the news, but a little confused. I told them I was switching my degree. If I was going to stick it out for two or three more years of school, at least I was going to do it on my own terms. A degree was a degree was a degree, and I could parley an Arranging and Composing diploma from Berklee into a teaching gig if I had to, at least that's what I told my parents and they bought it.

Looking back on it all after forty-something years, and seeing the benefits an education has given me, it's easy to see that I made the right decision. At the time, however, even after my revelations, I was still racked with doubt. I didn't sleep much that night and was a nervous wreck the next day as I made my way down to the studio where we were finishing up some last minute recording.

"Well, did you decide what you want to do?" asked Van as soon as he saw me. "You want to come with me?"

"I'd love to, Van, I really would," I answered, finally able to put off the decision no longer. "But I really have to go back to school and get my degree. I wish you the best of luck. Thanks for everything. It was great working with you."

Van understood. He kind of guessed I wouldn't be going with him. He knew I was just there for the ride, and like him, wasn't going to be deterred from my goal. And so it was over – almost.

Chapter 22

The Party

Soon after our recording sessions one of Van's backers held a party for him at his house in Cambridge to celebrate his new record contract. It was a large, stately, Victorian mansion with enough rooms to house six families in style. Three floors of amazing art collections and antique furniture, it had a complete discotheque and game room in the basement.

Until this time I never realized Van had backers. That must have been how he could pay us even when no one showed up. Van was shrewd. He not only knew how to perform on stage and write songs, he knew how to handle the complex business end of it, the wheeling and dealing, the phone calls and meetings with lawyers and producers. And here I thought he could barely carry on a decent conversation. Shows you what I knew.

I arrived together with Tom. I had on my brown velour Nehru jacket, my best pair of bell-bottoms, and my new leather boots, all purchased while Victor the one-armed drummer was auditioning for my job. The place was full of expensively dressed adults and teenaged girls, none of who were over seventeen if they were a day.

The house was exotic to say the least. There were richly furnished rooms and fern-crowded dens. The game area came complete with billiard table and stuffed animal heads. It was like out of a dream or some movie lot. There was a porcelain chair from Bach's time and priceless heirlooms hanging from the walls. One room had a dentist's chair complete with drills and spitting basin. I've already mentioned the full-blown discotheque in the basement, with a DJ's booth, swirling lights, and an ear-shattering sound system, full of kids shaking their booties.

I did my best to mingle and carry on a conversation, but after a while most of the adults ignored me. I noticed Van in the kitchen whispering something into a young girl's ear. She blanched, turned red, and hurried away. He just stood there with an unperturbed expression and sipped his beer. I wondered what he said and began looking for someone's ear to whisper into. It didn't take long for her to find me.

"Don't sit there!" she warned as I was about to sit in the porcelain chair. I had been eyeing it with the obvious intent of trying it out.

"It'll probably break if you do," said the attractive teenager. "It's from Bach's house." She had a perfect face and soft black hair. Dressed impeccably, she looked much older than her sixteen years.

"No kidding," I replied, comfortable now I was with someone of my own intellectual level. "Bach was great! We're studying his fugues this year in counterpoint class."

I got the distinct impression it was her place. We walked into the next room, the one with the dentist chair and the ferns. It reminded me of the living room in the Addams Family.

"You play with Van Morrison, right?" she asked.

"Yeah, I'm his drummer."

"Cool!" she said. She gave me a tour of the house, pointing out all the works of art and fine paintings as if she had purchased them herself. Although the place was packed with musicians, businessmen, and their wives, as well as teenagers of all shapes and sizes, I felt completely alone with this beautiful, enchanting young lady. I certainly didn't see any nervous parent watching us, although I'm sure there must have been one there somewhere.

I asked her if she wanted to go out.

"Elvira Madigan is playing down at the Charles Street Theater, if you want to go?"

"Sure," she said. She seemed quite eager to go out, a rarity in my pathetic social life, especially with a girl so pretty. She must have driven the high school boys crazy.

We wandered to the kitchen were Van was standing with a few of the adults, probably parents and backers. Who knows, perhaps one of them was this beauty's parent. If they were, no recognition was made. She didn't seem interested in Van. He may have already whispered in her ear for all I knew.

She said she was going to college in the fall, but if so she'd have to be some kind of child prodigy. I've met mature, sophisticated fourteen-year-olds you'd swear were nineteen, but this young thing could not have been over sixteen. I played along, flattered that she would lie for me. I was usually the one doing all the lying.

I'm afraid I monopolized her time all evening. She was hypnotic and full of interesting conversation, not the usual type of teenage banter. Until I met her I was bored to tears, the minutes dragging by so slowly they seemed like tiny hours. After Tracy appeared time literally flew by. Before I knew it Tom and the guys were leaving, and unless I wanted to walk home it was time for me to go as well. Sure some protective mother or chaperone was going to whisk in and sweep her away, I said goodnight and made sure to get her number.

I knew she was too young for me, unless I was willing to wait two or three years. Still I was intrigued.

I ended up calling her a couple times before our date, just to talk and get to know her. She seemed nice and was anxious to go out. Later in life I would learn that a three or four year difference between a man and a woman is nothing, and is in some ways ideal. Back then, however, the thought of dating a girl that young, with me about to enter my junior year in college and my twenty-first year of life, just didn't seem worth the trouble. Three years is a long time to wait. What a fool! I don't know, maybe it was the thought of sitting through three hours of Elvira Madigan again. In the end I did her a favor and canceled our date, telling her one lie or another. I never bothered calling after that. I hope I didn't break her heart, but then again, I was almost a rock star and breaking hearts is what you do.

Chapter 23

Astral Weeks

So Van was on his way to a new, highly productive phase in his life, and was done with Boston and yours truly. We did a final gig on the Cape that weekend, just like we started twelve weeks before, a fitting end to a memorable summer.

Where I thought he was leaving Boston to go out to the west coast to cut the record he was actually going to New York, but I wouldn't learn that until years later. He actually stayed around town for a couple of weeks playing with an acoustic band at places like the Catacombs with Tom Keibania and John Payne, honing new material before going to cut the groundbreaking *Astral Weeks* album. I was totally oblivious to all this being caught up in my own little world, getting ready for school and finding a new apartment, preparing to work my way through the last two years of college.

Had I known Van was playing in the Catacombs, right next to school with Tom and John, I would have stopped by and sat in. I would love to have done an acoustical jazzy set with him! Instead, I was jamming in the band rooms at Berklee with cats like Richie Cole.

That year I got my wish and played with some of the best musicians in the school. You never knew who was going to show up in one of these pick-up sessions. I sat behind the drums one evening and wouldn't you know, Miroslav Vitous, the bass player, was sitting right next to me. He was so tall and his hands so large, he could sit on a low stool and play the thing almost like a cello. He was just a kid at the time, with long curly hair, but boy could he play. I mean his hands just dominated that big bass fiddle. He owned that thing even back then. He played so effortlessly. He was already well-known before he got to Boston, one of those guys with a crowd by the door during his audition. After we played a few tunes he looked over at me and smiled.

"You listen well," he commented.

"Thanks," I said, and put down my head to concentrate on the next tune. Playing with Vitous was like floating on air. I worked with his bass as if it was part of me, comp'ing the time on the ride cymbal, while I offset the accents on the snare with my hi-hat and bass, making the time just slide by.

One day in another pick-up session at school I looked up from my drums to see this Indian-looking dude standing there with a tenor hanging from his neck. It turned out to be Ernie Watts, who was at Berklee on a Downbeat scholarship, although I didn't know it at the time. I just knew he was another one of those guys everyone crowded around to hear audition.

What a session. I still remember it to this day as a highpoint in my musical life. It's so easy to play with people like this. They just take you and carry you along. It was incredible. By that time, when I was on, I played as good as anyone. Playing fusion with Jack, I'd get into a zone where you'd swear Tony Williams was sitting in, the same with straight-ahead jazz. I was developing a modern style of my own, based on the drummers I loved and listened to, like Elvin Jones.

After a few bars of the first tune, an up-tempo Coltrane song, Ernie looked up from his horn at me. It was a moment of acknowledgement that I instantly understood. It was a look of approval. I was on that night, sounding just like Elvin, kicking with his licks as he played with the time. Man was that sweet. There were a dozen students hanging outside the practice room door digging the sound. That one jam-session did more for my reputation at school than playing with Van all summer. It was magical. A few months later I turned on the TV to see Ernie playing the same amazing tenor solos with the Tonight Show band. You just never knew who you would bump into at a jam session in Berklee.

I also got to study arranging with Herb Pomeroy that year, and drums with Alan Dawson later on. In addition, I got deep into my music composition courses. All of a sudden I wanted to be a serious composer like Bartok and Stravinsky. Just another spurt of latent talent and creativity that led nowhere, but at the time the world was bright with possibilities.

I'm sorry to say I almost completely forgot about Van, except when one of my friends like the Keatings or Joy and Judy dropped his name to impress someone. It's only in hindsight that those days working with Van stand out so vivid and special. That first semester back at school as a Composition major, however, Van was no longer on my radar screen, at least not initially.

A few months later, around November, Van came out with the *Astral Weeks* album. My new roommate, Glenn Adams, another Berklee student, bought the record and showed it to me. We were living on upper Commonwealth Avenue in Brighton at the time, with my brother Jim, who was a bass player and also going to Berklee. Glenn was miffed that it wasn't a rock album and was going to take it back to the store to get a refund. I bought it from him for five bucks.

Two things immediately struck me about the album. First, there were all jazz musicians playing with him, as a matter of fact, the Modern Jazz Quartet minus Milt Jackson the vibeist. Secondly, Tom Kiebania, my good friend from the year before was nowhere to be seen. I wondered what had happened to him. I had images of him being stranded somewhere in the middle of the country on his way to LA with no friends or money. That's what he got for going with Van. I felt partly vindicated. I had indeed made the right decision, but at the same time was saddened. What had happened to my friend? I have been wondering that for the past forty years.

Then around ten years ago I read a biography of Van called *Van Morrison – Can you Feel the Silence* by Clinton Heylin. Wouldn't you know, there as big as life was a picture of Tom Kiebania playing bass in the Catacombs with Van. The book is full of great quotes from Tom. It's funny, for thirty-five years I thought Tom had dropped off the face of the earth, but I was the one who had disappeared.

I wouldn't say the book itself is very flattering to Van – Morison did everything in his power to keep it from being published - but it has a nice chapter about that summer when he was in town playing with Tom, John, and me. It really captures the time and seems accurate for the most part, except where Tom said that I quit the band because my lease ran out and I had to go back home - so much for the facts. They even added an extra 'e' to my name, but last time I looked Bebo was still a four letter word. Actually, Tom was partially right, the lease on my Gloucester Street pad had run out and as I've said, I was focused on renting another apartment and getting ready for the new school year, where I would be supporting myself.

I can't really blame Tom for getting the story wrong. We totally lost touch. We saw each other practically every day and hung out together in the evenings, and then suddenly he was gone. I never saw or heard from him again until a short time ago, almost forty-six years later when he found me on Facebook.

With my self-centered focus and altered sense of reality, I got things totally mixed up. For some reason, even though I had the jacket cover right in front of me, I thought the name of Van's album was *Astral Wings* and that it was recorded in LA. It was only after reading Heylin's book that I learned it was done in New York and what the real name of the thing was. And that they had played at the Catacombs without me! I'm not sure what *Astral Weeks* means. *Astral Wings* still seems to fit the music better to me. Then again, I never listened to any of Van's lyrics, even when I played the vinyl, which I did several times. I was too focused on the musicians and what they were doing.

The album was an incredible breakthrough and totally unexpected. I knew we had sounded jazzy on the tapes and Van was a big fan of the genre, but I never expected him to come out with anything like this. He was accompanied by three of the biggest and most respected names in the business, Connie Kay, the drummer, and John Lewis, the piano player from the Modern Jazz Quartet, together with one of my favorite bass players, Richard Davis. I couldn't believe it! I mean, this was as straight-ahead jazz as you could get, and it was Van doing it! I can't tell you how cool I thought that was.

Although we played a few of the tunes on the album with the electric band that summer, they were almost unrecognizable. He must have worked on a lot of them after I left. As much as I admired the effort, I couldn't help thinking he sounded better playing with Tom, John, and me. We definitely would have given those tunes a little more of an edge, a bit more energy. I might be prejudiced, but the Modern Jazz Quartet without Milt Jackson on vibes just didn't do it for me.

When I first listened to it and during the subsequent years, I wondered if it was really Van who produced it or the studio cats. In the end, I think it was the record company who called the shots and had their guys do the date with their own arrangements – and who can argue with Richard Davis over Tom Kiebania, or Connie Kay over Joe Bebo. But when Van finally had a chance to fashion things his way with the next few albums, you could tell the difference right away. I like to think that the band that played with him that summer of '68 had some influence on those later records, especially songs like *Domino*.

You can hardly turn on a radio today or watch a movie and not hear one of Van's tunes. I stop whatever I'm doing and listen when *Brown Eyed Girl*, the song I used to hate, comes on the radio. And when I hear his distinctive voice on a movie soundtrack I'm instantly transported back in time wishing I was on the stage with him playing that song. You know the song that you heard on your honeymoon or dancing at the prom with your first love, your favorite tune. Almost every one of Van's songs is like that to me.

I can't tell you how many times over the years when Van has come to Boston I was this close to going to see him. The thought of being subjected to a possible snub, however, was just too much for my fierce, misplaced sense of pride. I guess I just don't see myself as one of those people who go back stage. I should have made the attempt to get in touch with him, if only to let him know how much I enjoy his music, but I always felt I had let him down when he asked for the last time if I wanted to go with him. Not only that, but I'm a civilian now, having turned my back on the music he's given so much to over the years.

Until quite recently I had no idea that Tom almost made it onto *Astral Weeks,* although I recall that John Payne, the flute player from Berklee, played on a few of the cuts. Tom actually showed Richard Davis the baselines for the songs. How cool is that to have on your resume?

I often wonder what my life would have been like if I had quit school and gone with Van. I certainly never had another opportunity like that, or ever again got so close to fame. Would I have gotten on the recording? I doubt it. I more than likely would have sat on the sidelines like Tom. One thing for sure, my life would have been different.

Chapter 24

Life After Van

I graduated from Berklee with a degree in Arranging and Music Composition in 1971 after three more years of school, the result of changing my major. The extra year was a burden on my family, but I was making enough money to help share the expense, and my grades were good enough that no one complained. There's a great picture of me at graduation shaking the hand of the music legend, Duke Ellington, who had always been one of my idols as a kid - although I'm a Basie man at heart. My dad was in the audience with my mother and the rest of my family, who all came down to Boston for the occasion.

When my father shook my hand afterward, I could tell he was proud. His eyes were moist and full of love. After all, his lifelong dream had come true. His son had gotten a college degree, the first in the family. My dreams were still before me.

After graduation I stayed in Boston and worked around town playing, teaching, and writing. I was fortunate to hook up with some talented musicians in the area after I left school, rooming with Harvey Swartz, the bassist. We lived with two other gentlemen, a keyboard man from Bronx, NY, named Andy Leverne, and a sax player, also from New York, named Larry. Neither had gone to Berklee, but Andy was a monster, just an incredible pianist and great fun to jam with. He went on to play with the Arti Shaw Band and other big name groups, and has had a very successful career as a keyboardist, composer, teacher, and recording artist over the years, like many of those who came by to play music with us.

The house became the jam session center. Musicians from all over would drop in to play. Two of my favorites were Jerry Bergonzi, the tenor saxophonist, and Cladio Roditi, the trumpeter. Jerry used to like to play with just the two of us, an unusual dual. He liked the way I worked the time and followed him.

The place would come alive when Cladio came by with his entourage, which included the sax player, Victor Brazil. Names like Darius Brubeck and Sammy Nestico would visit, although I'm not sure who invited them. That was kind of cool, but our local boys, Andy and

Jerry, would put these guys to shame. My friend Harvey was no slouch either.

When I first met Harvey Swartz, our first year at Berklee, he was a piano player. Somewhere along the line, around that summer of '68, Harvey switched instruments, transitioning from a rather mild-mannered, conservative piano man to a wild, long-haired and crazy bass player. Suddenly you'd see him rushing around the school carrying his big fiddle. I never saw Harvey without his instrument after that. Every time I'd see him, in the dorm, on the stairs, in the lobby, on the street, Harvey would have his bass. By the time we were living together, in just three years, he became one of the most sought after bassists in the area. He's not only since recorded and performed with the singer, Sheila Jordan, but has gone on to have his own recording career as Harvey S.

That creative year culminated in a weekend at Lenny's on the Turnpike with Mose Allison, the great blues singer, songwriter, and piano player, and another personal idol of mine as a teenager. Harvey Swartz was playing bass. I was sitting in for Alan Dawson that weekend, so got to play on his drums. What an honor.

Playing with Mose Alison was a fun experience and another highpoint in my short musical career. He gave me a drum solo every set. Trading fours with Mose Allison is like trading stocks with Warren Buffet. It just doesn't get any better than that. I heard that Van was also a big Mose fan and did a tribute album to him years later. They even gigged together! Now that's a bandstand I would have loved to be on!

Harvey and Andy ended up going to New York when our lease ran out. For the second time in my life I ended up bagging out of leaving Boston for the Big Apple.

If you wanted to make it in jazz, New York City was the place you had to be. My few experiences in the great metropolis left me cold and longing for the relative tranquility of quaint Bean Town. I had no desire to pull up stakes, leave my comfortable lifestyle, and go down to the City to hang out. Going to jam sessions, sitting in with bands in nightclubs, hanging out in all-night joints, practicing my axe in some cold, damp basement all day, all for the hope that some big time band leader would give me a break and hire me for a recording or tour, was just a little too risky for my blood.

I didn't mention all the drummers who came by the house, some damned good ones too. At times, when I was on, I sounded as good as anybody behind a kit. I mean, hearing back the tapes sometimes I couldn't believe it was me. I sounded just as good as the cats I listened to on vinyl. I had a way of working with and off the other musicians that was unique, and could make it burn, but I never knew how I was going to play when I sat down. Sometimes I'd sound amazing, everything working on its own, following and kicking with every subtle nuance of the other players, the drums sounding perfectly tuned and crisp, the skins alive, my hands and feet working together of their own accord. Other times I'd really scuffle, my hands not syncing with my feet, the drum heads feeling dead, the sticks as if they were made of lead. I just never knew which it was going to be.

Then there were the times during our sessions when everyone would take twenty minute, sometimes thirty minute solos. The songs would seem to go on forever while everybody played a solo through fourteen choruses. I didn't want to stop and let some other drummer play. I wanted to play something different, get into another groove with some different sounding changes, rhythm, or tempo.

It was then that I realized, as I had to make yet another decision whether or not to go to New York, that I really didn't have the soul of a jazz musician. I couldn't dedicate my every waking moment to one thing, my instrument, like Harvey and Andy did, or Richie Cole. As a matter of fact, almost all the guys who ended up going to New York and making the big time were obsessive. All they did was play music, practice music, listen to music, talk about music, or work on their musical instruments, making reeds, filing bridges, tuning keyboards. Anyone who could play a half hour solo is got to be a little bit self-absorbed. Even I wasn't that self-indulgent.

So I stayed in Boston, played around town, taught sundry things, and partied with my friends. Somewhere along the line I stopped playing jazz and became a top-40 drummer, doing music where there were no long solos, the work was steady, and best of all, there were dancers.

I supported myself through the years working in club bands while I tried to become a serious composer of 'legitimate' music. These groups were usually headed by a husband and wife team or some amateur musician with a day job. We would work anything from a Holiday Inn on the turnpike to the Playboy Club in downtown Boston. I did it all, working as a free-lance musician around town.

I loved playing for dancers, probably a throwback to my days backing up strippers. There's nothing like people grooving on the dance floor to your music. Even with these club-band amateurs I played with some excellent musicians, guys who could make the most average husband and wife duo sound like Las Vegas stars. I mean some of those bands would rock the house.

I worked in one group with a rhythm section that it was impossible to sit still to. We were backing up a female singer – we called her the wife of Dracula because of her striking but gaunt look – and her guitar-playing husband. She had a good voice and worked hard on stage, while he knew the chords and strummed along to the beat, but the sidemen they found were incredible. The bass player, from Mexico City, a guy named Fernando Beltrane, was actually a classical cellist by trade. Not only was he an incredible musician, he was an amazing person, intelligent and fun[5]. The keyboard man's name was Rick Martinez, from New York City, I think. Boy could they rock. When Rick and Fernando and I got that Samba thing going, there wouldn't be a person left sitting in the house. We could drive a beat so hard you just had to get up and dance. Rock, Top-40, standards, or Latin, it didn't matter. I'd pop that backbeat so solid you'd think the saints were coming, stick snapping off the rim of that snare, the bass drum kicking off that, we'd vibrate that beat into the floor. The place would be filled five nights a week when we played, with the whole room packed on the dance floor boogying. Man did I have fun playing dance clubs with Rick and Fernando.

Working in night clubs, while it may not have been the most edifying way to make a living, had its good points. I had my days free; I got to play with some surprisingly good musicians; and best of all, I met my wife, Kathy, while playing in a hotel club and steakhouse in Revere.

I say staying in college was a life-changing decision, but meeting Kathy is what really changed my life – for the better. Although a wee bit younger than me, she was much more sophisticated and worldly, despite all my experiences as a rock star. She liked jazz and had seen

---

[5] Tom thought I was a good chess player because I would show him the openings, but Fernando could play two of us sitting in the corner with his back turned away from the board and beat us every time, and he had a teacher who could trounce him just as easily. It just went to show me the incredible levels of human achievement. No matter how good you think you are at something, there is likely someone, somewhere, who is that much better. But if you work hard enough, you may look up one day and find that you have become one of the best, so never stop trying.

most of my idols live on stage. She was a girl after my own heart who won my heart the moment I met her. It was love at first sight and a struggle to finally win her hand in matrimony.

As an out of work musician – as fate would have it we met on the last night of the gig - I realized that winning her was going to be a challenge, but she inspired me, as they say, to be a better person. In an effort to improve my situation - as well as get an edge in the computer games we played – I taught myself programming using books borrowed from my friends and students. I had my own martial arts school by that time and many of my students worked at Digital Equipment Company in Maynard, Massachusetts, near where I lived and had my school, in Acton. I taught Chinese Kenpo and Jiu jitsu. I had a partner we called Pitt. Boy did we have a lot of fun.

It seems my whole life was focused on having fun and doing interesting things. Drumming, writing music, karate, computers, it was all just fun to me, a way of keeping busy. The lucky part is I've been able to make a living and survive doing what I enjoy.

Getting my black belt was another benefit of being a musician. It wasn't so much that I needed to defend myself – I've never been so much as looked at threateningly in a night club or bar where I played, and I've worked in some pretty rough places. But nobody ever messed with the band, unless it was the club owner. It was just that I had my days free and was getting kind of roly-poly. One night on the job I met a nice young couple who were studying kung-fu in Chinatown. It was during Bruce Lee's heyday, when David Carradine was kicking butt as Kane on TV, so the Arts were big at the time. I said if these people can do it so can I, and ended up with a black belt and a couple of tournament trophies after three years. I went to the dojo every single day and three nights a week, religiously. Let me just say drummers are good with their hands and feet. To make a long story short, a couple of my students who worked at DEC saw me writing programs in the dojo – Basic and Cobol at the time - and hired me to do some programming on the side for them, teaching me what I needed to know, like the Teco text editor on the Dec 10s, to get started. They ended up getting black belts from us – though we still beat the heck out of them - and I ended up with a job at DEC and eventually a master's degree in computer science. Not a bad trade.

I've done a lot of things since I've worked with Van, but all my later accomplishments were the result of staying in school and getting that degree. It not only gave me the discipline to see a thing through to the end, but the confidence to know that if I could do this, I could do other things as well. I was able to use credits from Berklee as prerequisites for graduate school in Computer Science at Boston University. It all stemmed from that fateful decision in the summer of '68.

As anyone will tell you, the prime purpose of college is to teach a person how to learn. Once you know that, whether it's at BU, or MIT, or Berklee College of Music, or your local State University, there's no stopping you. No one told me that when I was seventeen and if they had I probably wouldn't have listened to them, but I'm glad I listened to that little voice that told me to forget the fame and finish my education.

No matter where I go or what I do, I'll never forget that memorable summer of '68 when I became a part of music history, however small and insignificant. Working with Van Morrison, making music and learning about life was the ultimate adventure. That experience will stay with me long after most others have faded.

I can't help feeling John, Tom, and I had some impact on Van, although he probably wouldn't admit it. He was at a crossroad in his life, a turning point. There were 3000 miles between *Gloria* and *Brown Eyed Girl*, and light years between those songs and what we were playing. I can't help thinking that the three of us had some influence on him and his music. You can't really hear it in the Astral Weeks album with the Modern Jazz Quartet's smooth West Coast sound, but in some of Van's later recordings it's more obvious. The decision to opt for my lighter, jazzier sound during the demo-tape sessions may have set the tone for some of his later productions - who knows?

We were just a group of guys who wanted to make music. We could be loud and raucous like in the skating rink in South Deerfield, or soft and jazzy as at the Catacombs. The three of us had a unique, rhythmic, energetic blend, and Van, with his distinctive voice would be right there with us, head down, eyes shut, blowing his harp or moaning over the mic, just another player, and I loved him for it. *Domino, Moon Dance, Tupelo Honey*, we got to play these classic songs before anyone even heard them. You can imagine the thrill I get when I hear one of these tunes now, the memories that come flooding back. It only takes a half measure of the man's distinctive voice to take me there.

Tom Kiebania went on to marry his high school sweetheart, Claudette, the one we visited that hot summer day in Springfield. The girl I thought would break his heart gave him four wonderful children, two boys and two girls. They have ten grandchildren, the oldest of whom is a staff sergeant in the US Air Force. Tom, while not famous – although more famous and well-known than I may ever be – has been truly blessed. Though we lost touch for over forty-six years, I was not surprised to hear of his successful life because he had such a good heart, and things like that bear fruit.

Tom stayed with Van through the Astral Weeks album and after when Van moved to Woodstock, NY, leaving the band a short time later in early January, 1969. Tom was with Van when he played the *Café Au Go Go* in New York City, probably the highpoint of Tom's career. He continued to play music around his hometown where he worked in his uncle's printing company, recently retiring after forty-five years with a nice pension. Yes, Tom's had what I would call a charmed life.

John Sheldon went on to write and record with several famous artists over the years, including James Taylor. John still writes and performs music in Western Massachusetts.

Van Morrison's staying power has been incredible, as has been his musical output over the years, and he's still going strong. That is an amazing achievement in this world of latest crazes and the newest style. But good music never gets old.

There are only a handful of performers who have accomplished what he has. Van Morrison is one of the giants. There is not much I can say about the man that hasn't already been said and will be said again, except it was a pleasure working with him in all ways. He was a gentleman and true to his word, a man you could trust on stage and off.

My hat's off to both Van and John for sticking it out in what may be one of the most difficult professions in which to succeed. I continued to play professionally for ten years after leaving school, and for most of that time worked pretty steadily. I was able to support myself solely on playing and a little teaching – the karate school was fun but not profitable, at least not the way we ran it. But I didn't have a family to support like Tom soon did. The problem was that unless I had a steady gig in a house band somewhere – a fairly rare occurrence - I never knew where my next job would be, or if I'd even have one. The competition for work is another issue, and I'm not talking about a chair in the Tonight Show Band or the Philharmonic. I'm talking about a simple club band gig.

I never had a resume and don't remember ever dropping Van's name to get a gig. I doubt most of the people I worked with even knew that I played with the guy. I got most of my jobs by word of mouth, or from band leaders who'd come by the club to hear the group I was playing with. They'd steal a player in a heartbeat if they thought he or she would fill a club's dance floor. The problem was that for every one of them there were five drummers trying to grab my spot.

No matter how good I played, and I played pretty good in my day, there was always someone trying to take my place. Guys would actually use my drums to try out for my job. Just like a superficial lover or a used car salesman, always seeking something better, most band leaders I worked with were always looking for the next great bassist, guitarist, or drummer. There was little loyalty. Why should there be when musicians like me would drop a band for a better gig in a heartbeat, like I would have left Van if Charley Mariano had asked me to play with him.

Music is fun and exciting and for a few can be very rewarding, but it is a hard, cut-throat, thankless business and not for the faint of heart. I couldn't stand the uncertainty, and got sick of being the entertainer and never the one being entertained. My father had been right after all, computers were fun, and instead of being ten drummers for every seat there are ten jobs for every programmer. Yeah, I liked those odds, and Berklee College of Music helped make it all possible.

Thanks to my college degrees I have security and a comfortable lifestyle. Health insurance and retirement are not to be underestimated, and things even very good musicians, unfortunately, have to do without sometimes. You just never know where your next gig is coming from unless you are one of those lucky and talented few who have a solid studio job or made it big in the recording business. Like my dad said, one in a thousand.

Now as I look back on that summer forty-six years ago and my brief brush with fame, I'm struck with how fresh it all remains in my memory. It seems like only yesterday we were playing at the Tea Party and dying in the Supermarket; only a few years ago that I was banging out beats on stage behind Van's vocals, rehearsing songs in John's basement that would one day be hits; only a few summers ago that we were riding to the gig in the back of that blue van; in the summer of '68 when I learned anything is possible.

My Dad passed away in January 2005. He was seventy-nine years old. Dad built a wonderful life from literally nothing, but always regretted he never got to go to college. More than anything he wanted one of his sons to go. I'm happy I got to help fulfill his dream, and in doing so fulfilled my own. More rewarding than any benefit I may have had by staying in school is the fact that I didn't let him down when it came to one of the most important things in his life. That thought gives me much joy now.

He kept the picture of me shaking the Duke's hand during graduation, first in prominent display at the liquor store he owned and operated, then on top of the TV with Louis Armstrong and all his other best loved pictures. It made him proud and that made me happy. I've been very fortunate to get a chance to play, not only with Van, but with some of the greatest jazz musicians of our day. It was a privilege and an honor. So I want to dedicate this book to Sir Van Morrison and these other great musicians and composers and teachers, for their wonderful contribution to our entertainment, our culture, and our lives. Play on!

Not Quite the End

Author's Note

I had some qualms about writing this book. It is a departure from my usual fiction work, and writing about myself and my misspent youth was in many ways uncomfortable. Even though it describes my summer playing drums with Van Morrison, it deals with private matters and personal thoughts. Although autobiographical in nature, it has been fictionalized, as I reconstructed conversations I could not possibly remember after forty-six years, and tried to bring those times back to life.

I would like to apologize for the sex and drugs. Although not exactly edifying, if I didn't include these things I would only be telling half the story. As a twenty-year-old male out on his own for the first time in his life - who hadn't had a date in two years - the change in my social life is worth noting. What would a story about rock and roll in the summer of 1968 be without groupies?

Like the conversations, which in most cases I had to make up – except for Van's - although true to the actual situations, the drugs were also fictionalized. I have very little recollection of what we did and when, except for a few noteworthy occasions. However, it was part of my life at the time, and not including it would have made the story less real. I don't condone drug use, especially for young people, and am not particularly proud of what I did. Life is challenging enough without adding extra burdens like a drug dependency to drag you down. I was lucky and outgrew the taste for the stuff, but it could have turned out differently. Take my advice: don't take that chance. There are better ways to meet people and have fun.

Despite my misgivings about writing this book, and any embarrassment it may cause me, it is a story I wanted to share. I hope you found it entertaining, amusing, and true to life, and maybe even moving, as you followed me in my brush with fame and my coming of age, in the back of the van.

Made in the USA
San Bernardino, CA
19 November 2016